Be Angry, Sin Not.

Timothy J. Smith

A book in the Pearls of Life Series

Be Angry, Sin Not.

Copyright © 2018 by Timothy John Smith

All rights reserved.

ISBN 978-1-7322180-0-0

Merriam Webster Dictionary was our resource for definitions of "Feelings" and "Emotion."

Scripture taken from the New King James Version®.
Copyright © 1982 by Thomas Nelson. Used by permission. All rights reserved.

Scriptures taken from the Holy Bible, New International Version®, NIV®.
Copyright © 1973, 1978, 1984, 2011 by Biblica, Inc.™ Used by permission of Zondervan. All rights reserved worldwide. www.zondervan.com The "NIV" and "New International Version" are trademarks registered in the United States Patent and Trademark Office by Biblica, Inc.™

"Scripture quotations are from the ESV® Bible (The Holy Bible, English Standard Version®).
Copyright © 2001 by Crossway, a publishing ministry of Good News Publishers. Used by permission. All rights reserved."

Dedication

I dedicate this book to Jodi, my Bride, Lover and Friend. Jodi has encouraged me to write and share my story, to pursue the things in life that for many years I had not pursued, had forgotten I enjoyed, or had not had the freedom to experience. I am honored to be Jodi's husband, to experience life with her. I am a blessed man to have such a fulfilling marriage and rewarding life with her.

To my kids, you brought me all the joy any father could expect or ever hope for. I have said it before, here I place it in ink: "I am proud of you all, each of you alone is enough to make any father's life complete."

I must thank my wonderful sisters, Jane and Judi. My sisters have always loved and looked out for their little brother. Judi and I have been fortunate to live close to one another for the last twenty seven years which has allowed us to share more of our lives, the trials as well as the joys. Thanks, Dia!

My best friend Mike, you and I, are closer than brothers. We have shared life while making many memories. I love you and your wife, Judy, the "Granola Chick." Thanks for always being there and sharing the second half of life with Jodi and me.

I want to make sure I thank Deberah Williams. She worked as a partner with us, applying her talents in layout and design to help make this book a reality.

Special thanks to Glenn Eric Naylor for his illustrations. They added that extra something we needed to explain our message.

Contents

Introduction 7
Chapter 1: Be Angry 13
Chapter 2: Sin Not 25
Chapter 3: Angry? Not Me 31
Chapter 4: A Nightmare Triggered 45
Chapter 5: Secret Things 49
Chapter 6: Lessons from the Past 55
Chapter 7: Anger—Part of Life 63
Chapter 8: Getting Back on Course 73
Chapter 9: Masks 83
Chapter 10: The Great Commandment 87
Chapter 11: Self-Esteem ... Not! 99
Chapter 12: The Journey Begins 105
Chapter 13: Time to Retreat 111
Chapter 14: Choosing Calm 117
Afterword 125

Introduction

I was in the checkout line preparing to pay for my purchases when the cashier asked if my credit card had a chip.

I replied "No!" but then after a short pause added, "However, I used to have a chip on my shoulder."

The cashier was taken aback by my comment but intrigued. She then asked, "How did you lose the chip on your shoulder?"

I replied, "By dealing with my anger."

I am a regular guy. I am a husband, father, even a leader in my community and church. However, the person I am today is not the same Tim from years past. I was an angry person and anger influenced all of my roles. Today, I am still an ordinary guy but without the anger. This book is not about the theory of anger or even from education and training on the condition, but from personal and often embarrassing experiences from my life.

This book is written from the perspective of the one in the heat of the battle; a man trying his best to make a living and raise a family, a husband and father with the desire to leave a legacy when he dies. The person writing this book is not a Psychiatrist, Psychologist, Doctor, Counselor or Social Worker, just an ordinary man.

A guy with baggage he never knew he had or maybe he knew, but didn't take the necessary time or make the effort to address his anger. Maybe he did not want to acknowledge or own his baggage, believing if he did own his anger then he would be damaged goods—at least in his mind.

These were issues during my life I had struggled with for as long as I can remember. I thought my issues would go away over time or at the very least get better or work themselves out. I was wrong, but you do not have to be!

Anger won, everybody loses! This is exactly how I felt when I first realized how angry I had become. This was the moment when I became aware, for the first time in my life, that I could not remember a time when I wasn't angry. I could not recall a time when I was not charged—ready to explode. I realized how I had suppressed my anger for so long that I could not distinguish between feeling angry and being charged. I could not recall a moment in time when I was comfortable in my own skin, being at peace and rest.

When I share with others the realization of how angry I had become, I describe what I had done unconsciously with my anger for so many years in this way:

"There I stood at the front door of my home, almost paralyzed by the strong emotions deep inside of me. Behind that door was my family, the ones I loved with all of my heart. However, I knew I had to hide the real me in an attempt to protect them from what was underneath my surface persona.

So, I took a deep breath and opened the door leading to a large great room. Before I stepped over the threshold to walk into my home I would routinely, yet unconsciously, place my anger immediately inside the door of my life, under the wall-to-wall carpet where no one would see my anger." My anger would be hidden from everybody including myself. You know the saying, out of sight out of mind.

In the beginning, after putting my anger under the carpet, out of sight, I would then push my anger from the front door threshold all the way across the room into the farthest corner of the room. I subconsciously convinced myself that no one would ever know my anger was there. This was a means of compensation—a way of dealing with my anger.

I had learned to cover and suppress anger. This compensation technique had worked for a long time, or so I thought. I was able to hide my behavior, but not my attitude and certainly not my facial expression. Just ask my ex-wife, kids, and even my friends.

My means of anger compensation worked for a while, many years actually, until one day when I opened the front door to walk into my home and I fell flat on my face. My anger had tripped me and I was lying face down on the floor—embarrassed, hurt, and now even angrier.

The anger which, in the beginning I had pushed to the farthest side of the room, was out of the way where no one, including myself, would see it. My anger over time had now accumulated to such a mass it had come to the very entrance of my life. Anger, which I had suppressed for so long and never dealt with, had now altered and defined the person I had become.

I had become a man I did not like. A reflection in the bathroom mirror that reminded me of what I never wanted to become. This life-changing event scared me!

I was scared because for the first time in my life I was afraid that if I kept living life in this way I would end up old, lonely, alone, and bitter. It became apparent that this mass of anger "hidden" was actually only hidden from me. My family had seen it grow, watched me use most of my energy to suppress it and attempted to not disturb it—awaking a sleeping giant. It was a family secret no one wanted to acknowledge.

This book contains situations and circumstances from an ordinary man's personal life. My desire is it will provide insight into what anger is and where it comes from. Then use the understanding of anger to live a life where anger isn't just hidden away. Real, raw, honest examples and my personal failings shared are an attempt to help readers **DEAL with anger, not manage it**.

This book mirrors the context of my life. The "how" I lived the first thirty-plus years of my life, and the ways and methods I attempted to hide my anger or so I thought I had hid my anger. I put most of my energy into managing my anger—trying to convince everyone, including myself, that I wasn't angry. I fooled no one.

Here I share some examples of how I would justify almost everything I did. I became an expert at providing excuses for why I got mad, often blaming others for my behavior. I finally came to realize they were compensation techniques. Techniques I used as an attempt to make it appear as if what I was doing was for the benefit of someone else.

Honestly, I must admit, it was for my selfish agenda. My agenda of hiding my anger while appearing to others to be more confident and secure than I really was. How many of us can relate to that?

The content of this book comes from being vulnerable and openly sharing personal life situations which were often negative and destructive. Here I share personal accounts of my life experiences, the choices I made and the decisions which I came to, as well as the consequences of both the pains and rewards for those decisions and choices.

I will share with you lessons I have learned about Anger—Be Angry, Sin Not. These lessons are what I refer to as "Pearls"—valuable, precious gems which have allowed me to see beyond my anger to the underlying issues. My hope is that you will glean "pearls" from my vulnerability.

Chapter 1

Be Angry

Hello my name is Tim; I used to be an angry man. Life was not going as I had planned. My wife and I were having marital problems. Work was no longer as rewarding as it once was. Friendships just did not seem the same. When I spoke with my Pastor after my dad had died, I told him I felt as if I had issues. He counseled me to go looking. I told him I did not want to create more problems for myself. His response, "If nothing's there you won't find anything." I began my journey.

Be Angry! Yes, it is OK to be angry because anger is the proper response to being violated. Violation comes in many forms: physically, emotionally, financially, and even mentally. Physical violation needs no further explanation compared to the other three forms mentioned. Emotional, financial and mental violations are encountered from many avenues in many forms from what we would expect during person to person interactions to being violated in electronic media.

Being angry is not the problem. The problem comes when we do not control our anger or, for what many of us are guilty, letting anger control us. The behavior or actions we respond with as a result of our anger is what lead us to trouble. Our sin is the problem, not the anger.

The process towards emotional health is not a direct, short, simple trip. I compare this journey to riding a motorcycle versus driving in a car with the air conditioner running and a CD playing.

Riding motorcycles was one of the activities I had forgotten how much I loved. One day while I was sitting on my son's vintage motorcycle Jodi, my Bride, said "You look good on that motorcycle, you need to get one." I wasted no time and began looking to buy a motorcycle.

Today I ride twelve months a year. Motorcycle riders will tell you the destination is important but the journey is just as important, often much more so. When riding a motorcycle all your senses are fully engaged. You feel the wind, sense power as you roll the throttle, smell the scents, and experience the curves and pitch of the road while seeing scenery missed while riding in a car.

This is the journey you are about to begin. Each chapter is the beginning of another ride. New challenges, blind curves, sights and scents that take us back in time. Remember the destination is important, but do not miss the journey.

Many people believe to be emotionally healthy everyone's feelings must be spared; we must not make someone feel hurt. True emotional health is to acknowledge we have feelings and emotions and, with training and personal discipline, we can respond to our experiences instead of reacting without thought. We are truly emotionally healthy when we are in balance, homeostasis or at ease with our feelings, emotions, and our minds.

There will be times when we should and need to express our feelings and/or emotions. Feelings are defined in the Merriam Webster Dictionary as *3a: the undifferentiated background of one's awareness considered apart from any identifiable sensation, perception, or thought.*

Emotions are defined in the Merriam Webster Dictionary as

2c: a conscious mental reaction (such as anger or fear) subjectively experienced as strong feeling usually directed toward a specific object and typically accompanied by physiological and behavioral changes in the body. So as you work through this book, anytime the word *feeling* is used it is referring to a feeling not connected to a bodily response. Similarly, when the word *emotion* is used, it is referring to an intense feeling initiating a bodily response.

An emotionally healthy person's expression or response should match the experience encountered. A response which does not equal the experience is often the triggering of a "Pain body," a hurt once dealt with but has once again been triggered.

A pain body can be identified when an emotional reaction is greater than the experience warrants. The driving forces are a combination of the primary emotion not being completely resolved and anger triggering our "Fight or Flight" emotional reaction.

We must determine, while in a tense or crisis situation, is anger the first thing we feel or the second?

Those of us who struggle with anger will be inclined to believe anger is a primary emotion, the first thing we feel. When we remove ourselves from a tense encounter and reflect on our feelings and bodily responses there will be a core of three primary emotions.

The question which must be answered is whether anger is the first thing we feel or a secondary response coming out of a primary emotion being triggered? This distinction is crucial to be determined because this is the beginning of the process towards emotional health.

Think about the process when a baby is born. Imagine the fear experienced as it encounters the stark difference compared to the womb. As the baby goes through the birthing process, physical pain, hurt, is endured. Rejection is experienced as the baby leaves the comfort of the womb, and anxiety increases due to the unknown.

These are the primary emotions, the first things a baby feels—Fear, Hurt/Rejection, Anxiety. These are the first things we also feel prior to our anger.

Anger, being absent from the birthing experience, must be a secondary emotion resulting from a primary emotion being triggered. Therefore the three primary emotions are:

Fear is not an emotion many of us are willing to admit even in the direst of situations. I realized I had a fear of failure and success. Fearing I would be a failure when I attempted to accomplish something and failed my goal. Fearing I would be seen as a failure if I did accomplish a goal and then failed to maintain my success.

In the past I always thought of being **hurt** as a physical ailment. While I was teaching Anger Management Classes I would ask the participants what their idea of being hurt meant? The consensus of men in attendance described hurt as a physical condition and never in emotional terms.

One night while teaching an Anger Management Class for men using the visual of two individuals fighting I attempted a Martial Arts foot sweep. This is a Judo move used when you and your opponent are both holding onto each other while moving in the same direction and you desire to take your opponent to the mat. What you do is while you are guiding your opponent in one direction you sweep your opponent's feet out from under them in the opposite direction. With training, you are able to balance on one foot while simultaneously guiding their upper body into the opposite direction of their feet and controlling their fall to the mat.

The attempt was a success, but technique was missing. I was not prepared to support my opponent's weight. This was due to a lack of consistent training. Lack of training and I had pulled a hamstring two days prior to this class so I was physically compromised. Needless to say, both of us fell to the floor.

When we fell, my left side and ribs hit the table before I ended up on the floor. Being a man and not wanting to have my pride damaged I continued to teach the class, getting up off the floor and proceeding with the material planned for the class that night.

The next day I learned that I had fractured three ribs. The men attending that class could easily and readily identify that I was hurt. They saw me fall and hit the table, they heard the impact of my body come into contact with the table just before I ended up on the floor and they observed me lose my breath.

Emotional hurts or **Rejection** are not always so obvious. Once again the truth of: that which we do not understand or cannot name, we usually consider to be insignificant. Rejection, the emotional Hurt, is just as valid if not more so due to its nature and inconspicuousness. We often cannot identity or even name the rejection we perceive or experience.

The third primary emotion we experience is **Anxiety**. This emotion is so prevalent and increasing in our society today and one reason for the increase of our anxiety today is technology.

Technology, we would think, would provide us more time to relax and greater freedom but ultimately it does just the opposite. Today we learn of crises in real-time. We are seldom, if ever, disconnected from current events or our work. Even the continuous contact with friends and family can contribute to our anxiety because of the drama that often comes with relationships.

If we can identify and put a name to the emotion we are experiencing we then can deal with our emotion both completely and properly. When we experience a primary emotion and we do not address or resolve it anger will often emerge. We sometimes will identify being angry but we stop there; we do not seek a greater understanding of our emotions.

This means when we experience fear and do not address our fear or what I call "identifying the experience," the primary emotion will become lost and the secondary emotion of anger will often emerge.

When we encounter hurt or rejection and we do not work through "identifying the experience" of perceived or true rejection or hurt, anger will often emerge.

When we experience anxiety and do not validate our situation by "identifying our experience" anger will frequently emerge.

Anger is a secondary emotion. The second thing we feel. Our anger is triggered when a primary emotion is not completely and properly resolved.

Emotionally healthy people know how to take fear, hurt/rejection and/or anxiety and work through them, identifying their cause and resolving them so they can let it go. Sometimes the situation that caused a primary emotion to be triggered warrants anger. Abuse is a perfect example. Anger is not the problem—remember, Be Angry, Sin not. What we do when we are angry is what can lead to problems.

Think back to a baby being born. Anger is not mentioned, nor is love. Anger is a secondary emotion, as we have discussed. What about love? Is love a primary or secondary emotion? The first or second thing we experience?

Thankfully a baby does not remember the physical pain endured during childbirth. Once a mother holds her baby, gives love, the primary emotions of fear, rejection and anxiety are resolved. Research shows that when a baby does not receive this encounter of love attachment issues often follow.

Anger is a secondary emotion. Love is also a secondary emotion. Both occur in response to our primary emotions either being resolved or unresolved.

When we experience a primary emotion and then become angry we tell ourselves that we should not be angry. We often then find ourselves in the Anger / Love cycle. We become angry and we believe it to be wrong so we pursue love. We believe that being more loving is good and being angry is bad. We are compensating with love but with a love that is not pure. We love until a trigger exposes our anger and we remain in the unproductive cycle.

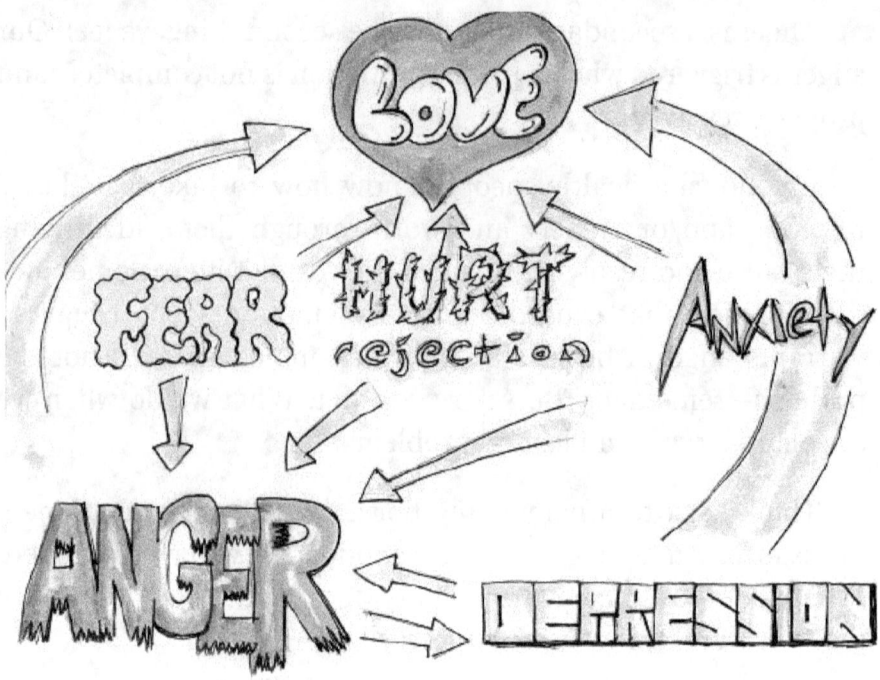

Anger, when unresolved, can drive us to depression which is often anger turned inward.

Love is a secondary emotion. Ask yourself these questions; If we have any unresolved fears in a relationship is there pure love? No.

If we have unforgiven hurt or rejection, even perceived hurt or rejection, in a relationship is there pure love? No.

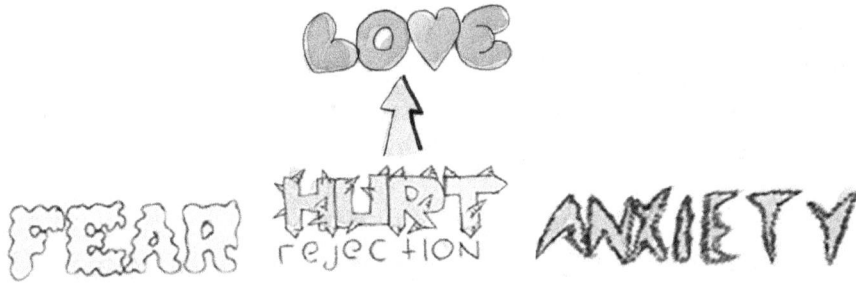

If we are concerned about the status, longevity or the direction of our relationship or we are anxious about our relationship today and its future is there pure love? No.

When we are without fear about our relationship, our hurts and rejections have been resolved, and we are no longer anxious about the status of where we stand, then we are able to experience the pure love intended for us. The love experienced especially in marriage when God said "Let the two become one." This is when we truly leave our past and cleave to one another.

When my wife and I would experience a core emotion but not admit it, I would engage my intellect to diminish the true loss I experienced. By continuing to do this later in life, I encountered even more devastating consequences.

Society encourages us to love in order to eliminate the negative experience of anger. If we feel good then our lives are perceived as good. By doing this we are putting on masks to cover up the real emotions we are experiencing, which compounds the problem. We must learn and train ourselves to deal with our primary emotions completely and properly in order to experience pure love and not just perceived love.

Here is an example from my life of when anger symptoms (secondary emotions) were my focus. I was an angry man who attempted to control his anger by internalizing it, managing it and not losing control.

This was the way both my ex-wife and I proceeded when dealing with difficult and uncomfortable issues. We would withhold our feeling while denying our emotions, not talking them through with each other or honestly admitting even having them.

We both had a lot of unresolved hurts and issues from our past. We believed enough love would make our issues go away or at least get better. The problem was that during our relationship we were not feeling loved and our needs were not being met. We were focusing on our secondary emotion of love, truly a symptom, and not the primary emotions of fear, hurt/rejection or anxiety.

Ultimately, the focus on the symptom of needing to be loved ended up with the perceived missing love being met through an affair. The affair resulted in the loss of many relationships within our family by various family members and contributed to divorce. We were two hurt and broken people wanting to be loved. Love was not the problem, nor was anger, both secondary emotions. The unresolved fear, hurt/rejection and anxiety emerged into a life of anger and destruction.

I realized I had never understood my anger because I never understood the primary emotions. I thought since I was not demonstrating anger in an aggressive way I wasn't angry. I was wrong. Now that I understand and work through my primary emotions I do not carry the charge I once did.

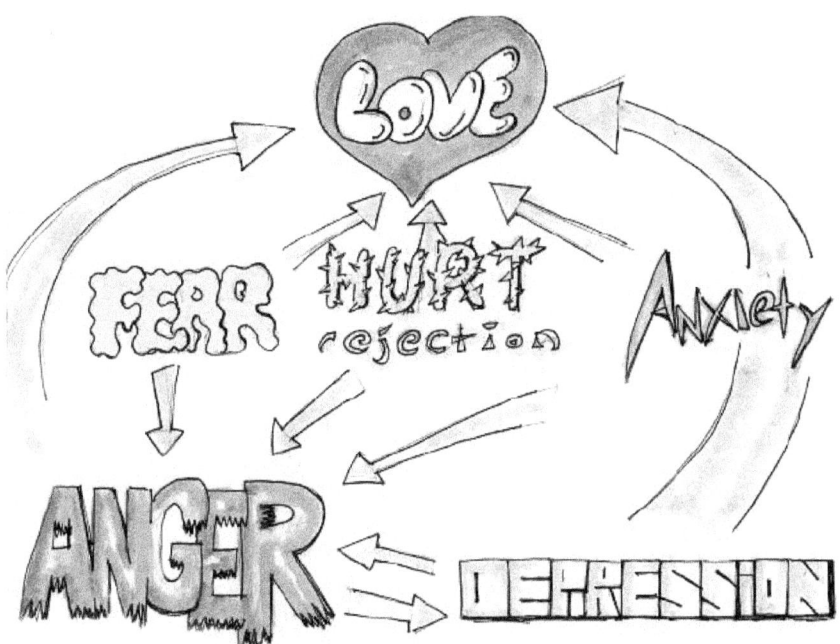

Chapter 2

Sin Not

Be angry, sin not. How do we do both? Good question.

Riding motorcycles is pure joy but the rider cannot become complacent during the ride, he must remain in control. Shortly after I began riding again my new bride, Jodi, decided she wanted to ride also. I told her if you want to ride, ride, but take a course first. I took the course with Jodi and although I did not have any major bad habits, I had several small bad habits that when combined, could become significant, contributing to an accident.

Sin is an archery term describing how far we missed our intended point of aim. When we have no filter by which we say and do things we will always miss our point of aim and sin greatly. Once we have a designated filter our aim is to never attack a person. Our intent is to address an attitude or a behavior. We are now prepared to be angry and sin not. Before having this perspective, I often believed Anger was a means to an end; falsely believing angry people win. When I realized the extent of my anger and the consequences I encountered, I began seeking answers regarding the idea of "Anger Won and Everybody Loses."

The very idea of anger winning is such a lie. Abuse, bullying, divorce, child custody, estranged family members, lost relationships are all evidence to the truth that anger never wins. Each of these situations has one thing in common—anger, and in each of these situations, everybody loses.

If "anger won" is used in past tense, it would be reasonable to experience a positive result in a present situation. I must admit I was not really winning at anything when I was angry. Are you winning anything with your anger? If your answer is yes, the next question is, "Really, what?"

If "anger won" is present tense, we could anticipate a positive future outcome as well. The problem with this reasoning is, just as our past is an indicator of our present, our present is a good indication of our future. If we are currently living in conflict or chaos, what would make us think the future would be different?

I recall a situation during one of my past management positions. There had been a loud argument regarding customer service and how some co-workers were doing their job. The argument was loud enough for the entire office to hear and Mike, my boss, wanted everyone to know that he was the boss. Following the heated argument, Mike walked into my office, sat down with confidence saying, "Well, I won that argument."

I told him, "Mike, you lost. You lost control and you lost the argument." My boss was fired the next day.

Focusing on the word 'won' the question is, what did the boss think he won? Winning an argument? Not likely. Just because someone does not disagree with you, does not mean they agree. Demonstrating who was in charge? At what expense? Losing your job?

Winning is one of the possible outcomes during times of adversity or even friendly competition. When I was an angry man I was no winner, even when I thought I had won. Later I realized my so called win was actually a loss. The angry person often uses his perceived strength of anger to achieve his goal, but the anger in many situations becomes a weakness.

I did end up winning after dealing with my anger. A win of learning that anger was only a symptom, a result of not knowing, understanding or acknowledging my core emotions. I was now able to experience anger and address an attitude or behavior without attacking the person. I was able to Be Angry, Sin Not.

Today life is a total win! I no longer just exist and push through life; I am actually thriving in life! In my past, the very concept of really enjoying and embracing life was so far from a reality I could not get my mind around the idea of looking forward to the next day let alone the next adventure. I was just barely holding on in life and would not even consider thinking or dreaming about the future. Are you thriving or just existing?

Here are some of the questions I had to ask myself and honestly answer in order to understand and deal with my anger.

1. Is my life seemingly full of adversity?

2. Do I feel as if life is a constant battle or a daily competition?

3. Do I always have to win?

4. Am I ever truly at rest and peace?

When I asked myself these questions I did not like the answers. I also came to the following realization:

When an angry person always has to win then the only reasonable conclusion a person can come to is that person's life is lived in relationships with losers. This means, if married they are sleeping with a loser. OUCH!

If anger never wins, and it does not for the long term, then the reasonable conclusion is that anger loses. When we unpack this concept it reveals how anger, when released, is now and will truly be devastating in our future.

Everybody is affected by anger not just loved ones but co-workers, family members, friends, acquaintances and even ourselves. Those who are angry are the greatest losers of all.

Taking responsibility for being the person responsible for losing at relationships is imperative. Being identified as the constant, the one person in multiple failed relationships with others is a beginning. Continually living life in this way the angry person will eventually be the only person without friends and estranged from loved ones. When we are angry everybody within our sphere of influence loses either directly or indirectly.

Losses—something lost, or we are experiencing a loss or we will experience one. The loss of consideration, the loss of respect, the loss of love, even the loss of relationship! These losses can be past, present or even future losses.

This is my story. Not a story for which I am proud but here I share what I have learned during my journey through life up to now. My learning took time, effort, and a willingness to accept the ugly and painful truth. I had to ask the questions many do not want to ask. Next I had to honestly answer them, and then deal with the consequences.

Being a regular person and like all of us my natural reaction is to avoid pain. I had to be ready and willing to overcome this tendency to avoid, mask, diminish, or even deny pain. I had to choose to work through the pain, not seek relief from the pain.

In one of the management positions during my career a policy was "Hire for character, train for ability." Building on this concept I believe it is a necessary character trait to learn to embrace and work through our pain. The pain we willing endure keeps us from doing more harm to ourselves and others. Harm that sometimes never heals. The process we endure often hurts, but hurting is most often temporary whereas harm is frequently lifelong.

My hope is that as we journey together through the sharing of these experiences and insights they will be beneficial for you to appreciate, maintain, and improve current relationships.

My desire is for you to gain personal victory over your anger. For you to learn about your core emotions and ultimately glean (find, own, and one day share with others) your **"Pearls of Life"**; pearls, or life lessons, which allow you to journey to the place of **"IN-TO-ME-SEE" (real Intimacy)**, first with yourself and then with the people in your life whom you love.

Chapter 3

Angry? Not Me

I never thought of myself as being angry. I could see anger demonstrated by others. I could even put a description to their actions as being anger related, but I would never identify the anger in myself. Realizing now that if I did identify my anger I would have considered myself as being flawed, less than perfect, damaged goods.

We never want to admit we are bad drivers or limited in our riding skills. When an accident happens it is always the other driver's fault. A recent report regarding motorcycle safety has documented that motorcyclists are poor at braking, need to improve making right turns, and although riders blame motorists, are just as liable for their accidents.

A common image of an angry person is the person who throws things, explodes, uses foul and vulgar language, is abusive to others through verbal put downs and demeaning speech, or their interactions with adults are as if talking to an infant or misbehaving child.

Anger and its many revelations are similar to addictions. Similar in that we may have a preconceived idea of the behaviors of anger just as we do with addicts. What it looks like, how it is displayed when people are angry, but anger like addiction shows its ugly self in many ways.

Some of us might have grown up believing that the person with an alcohol problem was the town drunk or the drunk you would see played on TV. Examples could be the drunk on the street or the classic brown paper bag wino living on the streets without contributing to society, the loser just living a minimal existence day to day.

Although this image may be true of a specific person with an alcohol problem, it is not all encompassing of alcohol addiction. The correct definition of an alcoholic is a person who struggles with the temptation, a person who cannot stop at one drink or for that matter cannot leave just a little alcohol in the glass. The individual who struggles with alcohol may only drink one time a year, but when they do drink they become under the control of the alcohol, and ultimately relinquish their own self-control.

Addictions are more common in our society today than many are willing to admit. We all have our struggles. Some struggle with personal significance so they attempt to be recognized always pursuing the elusive moment of fame. Some struggle with achievement so the acquisition of titles and things is a priority. Others struggle with acceptance so love, sex and relationship addictions are the means of compensation.

We all have our struggles and we all have our strengths. One very important reality learned, which came out of a time of brokenness, is often our strength may become our weakness. We have a tendency to gravitate towards our strengths; we begin to rely upon them no longer pursuing personal growth and maturity and soon what was once our strength becomes the means to our destruction, our strength becoming our weakness.

People who are angry may not even realize they have a problem. They may have the same misconceptions that I had, or they may be comparing themselves to a false definition of anger. This false definition may have been self-formulated out of a sense of self-preservation or through their personal life experiences. Hopefully, by now your preconceived thoughts and perceptions of anger have been challenged. Together let us explore and learn a true and realistic definition of anger.

All experts agree anger is an emotion. This is seemingly a very straightforward definition. When we unpack this statement we can learn even more.

Anger is. This is part of the statement we must really get a grasp of. Anger will not go away. It was in the past. It is in the present. It will be in the future.

Anger is an emotion. Anger is not just a thought. It is not merely a feeling. Anger is an emotion. Anger is the emotion brought out by intense feelings, but at its core, anger is an emotion.

I always thought anger was just a feeling. This false belief was reinforced over the course of most of my life. I could not count how many times I heard from people who really cared about me say something like, "You are just feeling angry," or "Are your feeling angry?" or "Doesn't it make you feel angry?" The difference between feelings and emotions is that emotions have an effect on the body. These affect the body for good like self-preservation, or for detriment exhibiting in ulcers and other ailments.

I began to learn the difference between my intense feelings and my body's response to those feelings, what we identify as emotions. Emotions and feelings are very different but I always thought they were the same. How many of us have been told or it has been implied by our spouse and family members that they wanted us to be more feeling, more emotional. Feelings and emotions are somewhat similar but very different at the same time. Feelings are that, just what we feel at any given time. I feel tired. I feel hungry. I feel cold.

Emotions are when feelings become so intense that they cause a bodily response. Some examples could be when a child falls asleep in the middle of play from feeling exhausted. Our stomach growls or cramps because we have not eaten. We shiver or perspire depending on the ambient temperature or a recent encounter. These are bodily responses over which we have no control how our body will respond.

When anger (our secondary response to a primary emotion being triggered) is allowed to go unchecked people often experiences dis-ease (the body not at rest). Some symptoms might include stomach problems, back problems, depression (often anger turned inward) or any number of chronic symptoms. I had digestion problems and chronic heartburn. I also seldom woke up in the morning following a long night of sleep feeling rested.

We are all created by God with three distinct and mutually necessary abilities. These traits are what make us distinctly human and separates us from the rest of creation. The first ability for us to investigate is our **mind**, our intellect. This is our thought process, our reasoning ability. This thing called reasoning is what we do in our minds and can be applied independently of what we feel and even independent of our bodily response—emotion.

An example of an intellectual response independent of feelings or emotion would be if a person accidentally cut off his own finger, and this person methodically addressed the emergency by providing first aid to himself.

This intellectual response is what first responders are trained to apply in times of crisis. If these very special individuals had not been trained and developed the necessary disciplines required for a proper response to an emergency they would crumble in a crisis.

I had the opportunity to learn this so vividly during my career in the dental field. This is not a lack of sympathy for a patient, or even a personal attack, but a trained response to the emergency situation devoid of feeling or emotion.

During my career in the dental field I worked with Oral Surgeons and General Dentists treating their patients. Both are extremely competent in their chosen field, but usually approach treatment of the patients differently. In observation and training, a surgeon will always look for and identify a problem, a crisis to be solved, resolve the situation and go onto the next problem. The General Dentist will anticipate issues and have contingencies but usually out of a sense of reaction not as a trained anticipated response. These are two very different skill sets which were intentionally developed for their chosen specialty.

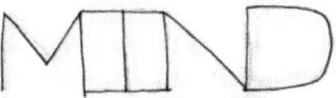

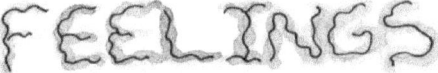

Feelings are very different from our mind or reasoning ability. For me feelings were always uncomfortable while reason was safe. That is why I always gravitated to or defaulted to my mind or reason or intellectual ability.

It's important to remember that feelings are always real, just not always accurate. You might say that someone hurt your feelings, but that may just be your perception. What they said was not what was heard.

From personal observations, women are often far superior to men when it comes to identifying feelings. From interviewing men I encountered while leading an Anger Management Class men can usually identify some feelings: mad, sad, bad, glad, happy, full, hot or cold. These feelings we choose to experience are also the very feelings we can choose to shut down just by using or defaulting to our intellect, our mind over what matters.

Some people can walk on hot coals without feeling the pain. This is accomplished by the individual's mere mental concentration or possibly from a lack of physical sensation. I knew a man who would hold a lit cigarette in the palm of his hand extinguishing it by making a fist; he did this without so much as a flinch. As do those people who walk on hot coals, my friend extinguishing a cigarette in his fist, they soon have scar tissue that develops in the area of continual harm being exerted to their body and soon they become almost numb to the experience.

Many of us enjoy experiencing our feelings to a certain level, but when feelings begin to progress to a bodily response or an **Emotion**, we intentionally shut down this progression.

When something begins to occur within us physically and we feel as if we cannot control it, or what we are experiencing is different and unlike anything we have encountered before and we cannot name it, or we feel we are losing control we intentionally shut the process down of feelings becoming an emotion. Women as a rule don't do this as frequently as men. Women were designed by God to be especially connected with their feelings and emotions. Let us look to nature and make some observations to validate this belief.

Women are much more aware of their feelings and emotions. Most women naturally go through a menstrual cycle every twenty-eight days. During this period they experience wide ranges of feelings and emotions. Women can discern when their cycle will start often just by feelings and bodily responses.

A woman following conception carries the child in her womb.

This gives the woman the opportunity to feel the baby move and kick, which in turn allows the mother to become emotionally connected with the child through the experience of pregnancy and then birth.

No man will emotionally experience these feelings nor will they ever experience the intensity. Men do not experience life as women—or a woman as a man. The testosterone and estrogen hormonal differences, the cultural expectations, and ultimately, although many today wish not to acknowledge, the intent by our creator God was for men and women to be different. Neither one is more important but both necessary and complementing to one another.

God has designed us to experience all three of his gifts:

Mind = our thoughts or reasoning process
Romans 1

Feelings = How we perceive things, often abstract and based on our senses. Phil 4:6

Emotions = our bodily response, frequently uncontrolled tears would be an example. Job, David, Psalms

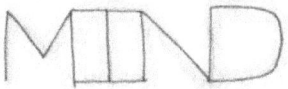

Learning that anger is an emotion we cannot put in a bottle to contain or place a label on it to sell is revealing. Unfortunately, today we have an entire generation that has not learned how to process these emotions because we have defaulted to the answer in a bottle—medication. So often we do not learn to process these emotions and we grow up emotionally deficient. Accepting this truth I needed to learn where my anger had come from and why. The only reasonable conclusion I could come to was we were created with the emotion of anger. Anger was given to us for a purpose. This was confirmed for me in scripture when we are instructed to "Be angry, Sin not." Ephesians 4:26

Many people want to deny their anger just like I did. When I denied my anger in reality I was denying a gift from God. Honestly, what I wanted to deny were my failures and the related sins which were the consequences of my anger. I was unable to separate the two, the emotion I initially experienced and the reaction to the emotion, my behavior and the consequences that followed.

Many have asked me during the classes I have taught, "If God is perfect and loving, why would He give us this negative emotion we call anger?" The answer is actually anger is not a negative emotion. It is what we do with anger which causes it to become negative and destructive. When we are filled with righteous anger or justifiable anger our body responds the way it was intended to respond, for self-preservation or protection.

This is truly a gift which we often dismiss. This positive response to anger is often referred to as the fight or flight response. When we are aroused out of anger the hormone adrenaline is activated within our body and brings about several automatic responses. With the production of adrenaline and its release into our system the bodily responds simultaneously from our eyes becoming dilated, the blood flow from our extremities gathers around our vital organs in the torso, our muscle's response time is quicker and they do not need our normal muscle recovery time, we experience greater strength, and a heightened level of both awareness and agility occurs.

These bodily responses were intended to protect us and help us to survive. With the increased quality of our living conditions and the almost elimination of threats to our very survival compared to the past we have lost our ability to discern when anger is being aroused and how to appropriately deal with its effects.

Participating in an exercise intended to demonstrate how we can determine if we may be under stress we learned if you place your fingers on your cheeks and ask yourself, "Are my cheeks warmer or colder than my fingertips?"—you will be able to determine your possible level of stress.

If both your fingers and cheeks are about the same temperature you probably are not encountering any stress, but if your cheeks are discernibly warmer than you finger tips (a noticeable difference) you are most likely encountering some form of stress, or disease, the body is not (dis) at ease.

The reason for your fingers being colder than your cheeks is an indication that the blood flow to the extremities has slowed, and the vital organs are being protected for the fight or flight response.

The illustration below represents the three gifts from God we are addressing.

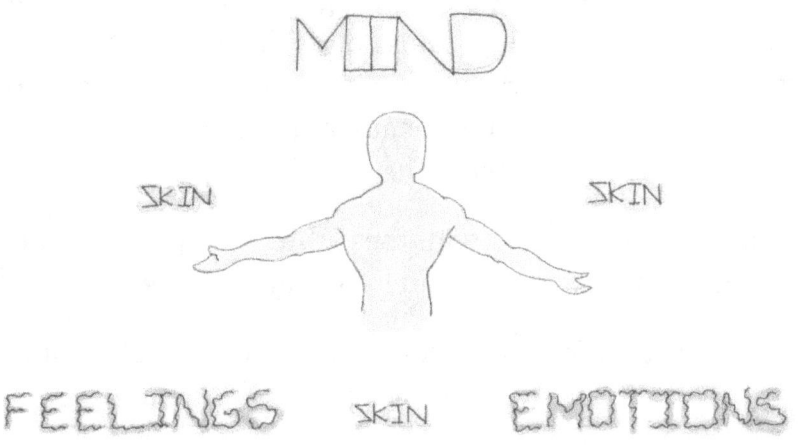

Realizing that all three of these aspects are interconnected with skin holding everything together, the cumulative effect is what makes us distinctly human having a soul.

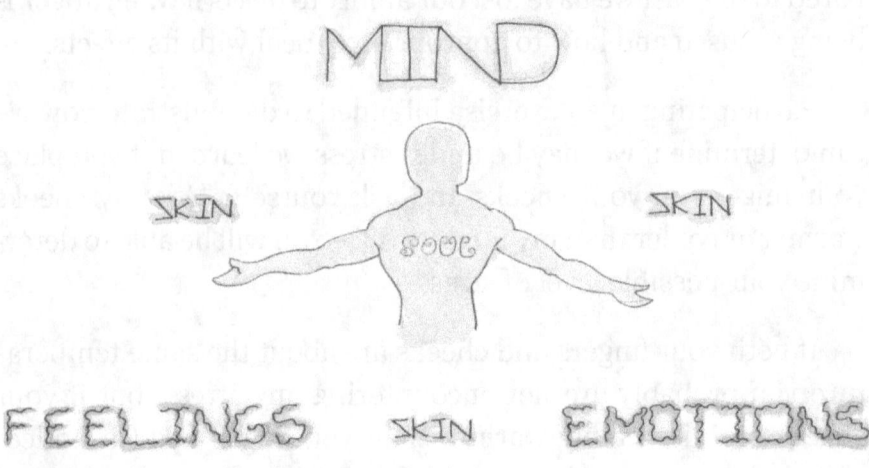

Most men have a tendency to dis-credit emotions just as I did while I was emotionally deficient. I did this because I did not understand or fully appreciate my emotions, and with the mindset my emotions must be insignificant, even silly.

Some people have issues with separating their feelings and emotions from their intellect or their ability to reason without the influence of emotions.

Both of these extremes are wrong and will have negative implications. We should hold those of us that default to our intellect or mind to a higher level of accountability because we often choose to shut down intentionally at the feeling stage, and we therefore will not experience the gift of emotion.

Personal experiences with these three independent but mutually connected aspects would look something like this.

See a girl, WOW—I like what I see. I intentionally change my behavior to pursue her, getting to know her better. I begin to spend time together and experience feelings. My feelings intensify and become more frequent and soon I feel this thing I do not know or understand. My body responds and I lose control so I intentionally take the path of least resistance to my mind and claim it must be love.

While I spend time with a girl I like, I begin to experience something I cannot describe. In my mind I attribute it to love shutting down my emotional experience.

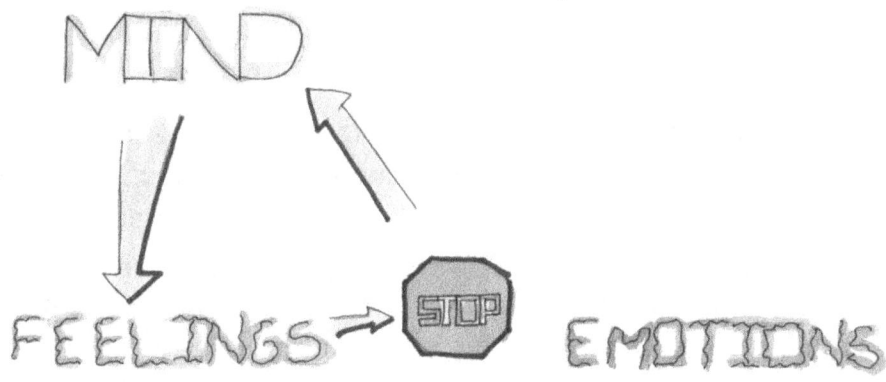

Here is another example. I am told my mother is to have surgery the week of Thanksgiving. This is not a time that people usually schedule routine surgery so this is not routine surgery. She enters surgery, initially recovers from the operation but has further complications and never recovers from the procedures and dies.

I experienced the loss of a loved one but immediately default to my strength, my mind, and rationalize that her condition and health was compromised due to alcohol abuse, smoking and years of abuse to her body. Rationalizing that if she had survived the operation her pride would not allow for her to be cared for or would have believed she would be a burden on others.

My mother underwent surgery which was deemed a success

although she never recovered. I attribute her death to her lifestyle, making reason overtake emotions.

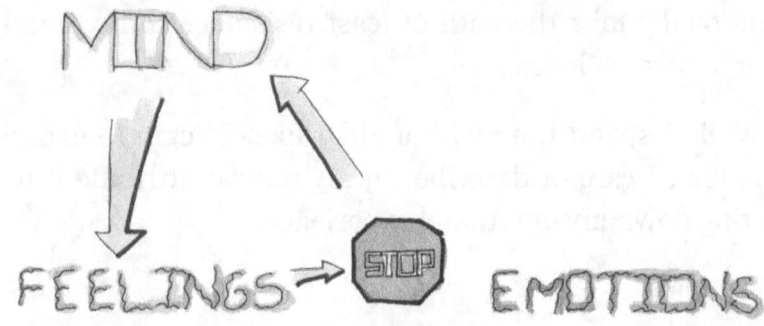

In these examples I began to feel something I did not understand and I intentionally defaulted to my intellect. I used reasoning ability to explain a feeling without experiencing the emotion. What I did out of compensation for being uncomfortable or being seen as foolish was gravitate to my strength—my mind. I lived this way for 35 or more years of my life, living between my mind and my feelings never honestly experiencing my emotions.

Emotions I would intentionally attempt to shut down out of fear of that which I did not understand. What I believe now is even more damaging and of greater significance, I denied a third of what God made me to be. I had been grieving God by not embracing my emotions.

A renaissance man I have become only by God's Grace. A man, who owns, embraces and enjoys my intellect, my feelings, and my emotions. The type of man I believe society needs more men to become.

A true renaissance man is the Knight (protector), the Loyal Companion (partner), The Scholar (learner), and the Poet (Romancer)!

Are you a renaissance person or do you want to be? More

importantly are you living and enjoying life as God intended? When was the last time you really let your tears flow and cried or when was the last time you laughed so hard your stomach ached? When was the last time you were in the Thriving Zone?

Chapter 4
A Nightmare Triggered

When I began riding motorcycles again I would often leave the house early on a Saturday morning and ride through the countryside. One day after my ride Jodi asked, "What memories did riding trigger?" I told her it reminded me of riding horses when I was a kid living in Tucson. I would ride the foothills of the Catalina Mountains experiencing the desert from the saddle of a horse.

I was traveling in Boston on a business trip when a nightmare of my past was triggered. The flight from Atlanta to Boston was uneventful. I was actually looking forward to my trip yet this experience brought back memories. Memories I had long forgotten. I was riding in a limo from Logan International Airport to my hotel where I would be staying for the week. I was traveling through the city by car service driving through the "Big Dig", a tunnel being constructed for better traffic flow.

Not long before my arrival to the city a section of the massive concrete ceiling had fallen onto a car crushing the occupants resulting in their deaths. The tunnel is intimidating by itself but with the lines of fluorescent lights, the curves with vertical changes, it is quite an interesting ride.

While I was experiencing the ride through Boston alone in the back seat of the car with someone else driving, being completely at the car service driver's mercy, a nightmare was triggered.

In the nightmare, I was falling down a tunnel. The tunnel had curves and directional changes, ups and downs. One minute I would be spinning, and then I would fall at different rates of speed depending on the terrain I envisioned. There were lights with no distinguishable origins and as I fell I would become more and more uncomfortable and uneasy. While I was free falling uncontrollably, the walls of the tunnel would seemingly close in on me. I would feel more claustrophobic the farther I fell. I felt myself cringing and coming almost into a fetal position as I was falling farther and farther with no end in sight. I was never fearful of hitting the bottom and dying. I was afraid of falling farther down from the last time I experienced this nightmare. I was fearful of losing my identity and never finding my way back.

I experienced this nightmare occasionally from the time I was ten or eleven years old through the first 16 years of my first marriage. It wasn't a nightly occurrence but frequently enough that every time I relived it, it brought both anxiety and anticipation. In my mind I consciously pushed myself farther down the tunnel in an attempt to learn why I was experiencing this nightmare. Every time I pushed I would descend a little farther but ultimately I would wake up.

When I awoke, I would be somewhat clammy, and definitely not rested, but certainly intrigued by what I had experienced. I always had the lingering question of why I had this nightmare, what did this nightmare represent?

Amazingly, I have not experienced this vision (dream or nightmare) since I began dealing with my anger. Anger I never truly realized I carried until the most devastating and rewarding time of my life. This moment was when I began the journey to becoming free, free from many things, especially free from anger.

Free from the anger that had consumed me and controlled my life. This was my secret nightmare. A nightmare I never shared even with My ex-wife.

Why share a nightmare? What significance does this have with anger? It is significant when a nightmare comes and we find ourselves awakening in the middle of the night. We have put the previous day behind us and we have not yet embarked on a new day. For many of us this is the only time we are not entertained by the multiple media platforms. We are not distracted by connections to our world. This is often the one time of day that we are actually being still without the need to be doing something. It is when we are being still our primary emotions often reveal themselves.

Do you have a secret nightmare? What are some of the dark hidden secrets of your life that, once revealed, will allow you to begin on your journey to peace and rest? We all have secrets, some are seemingly greater than others or so we think. From a medical analogy, surgery may be routine for the doctor and staff, but for the patient it is never routine. No matter how minor the cut, it is never normal to have a sharp object penetrate our body. Secrets are often like the wounds we encounter through life, we pass them off thinking they have little consequence but each penetrates deeper than we realize.

Chapter 5
Secret Things, Things Revealed

"The secret things belong to the Lord our God, but the things revealed belong to us and to our children forever, that we may follow all the words of the law." Deuteronomy 29:29

This is one of the first scriptures I ever intentionally attempted to learn and memorize. I had learned other scriptures but this one, this Old Testament relatively obscure scripture, really caught my attention.

What I learned from this simple verse was that we were never intended to know everything, even though I had placed an expectation upon myself to be well versed and more than capable in multiple interests.

This is true for every aspect of life including riding motorcycles. The most important lesson to learn regarding riding motorcycles is to ride at your ability. Frequently people will buy a motorcycle that is more powerful than they are able to control, bigger and heavier than they can handle, and they attempt to ride with riders who are far superior to their ability. Motorcycles are designed and capable to perform at a level greater than even the most experienced rider.

What a relief! Learning from our creator that I was never expected to know everything. Now I had the freedom to fail and if I did fail, I would not be a failure. Failure is an opportunity to learn a life lesson. I believe it is those times I failed that I have learned some of the most important life lessons. Often it is during these times that we grow the most and these are significant times of learning.

The things revealed to us are for us, and these revelations are from God. The things God has revealed to us are intended for us to learn and grow but ultimately intended for us to give Him glory. With this new freedom of not having to know everything but also with the understanding that God would reveal to us what we needed to know, I asked the question, "What is Anger?"

First and foremost, you must understand that I believe in God. I strongly believe our theology will carry us through whatever life holds. I believe in the God of the Scriptures, both the Old Testament and the New Testament. God is all knowing, ever present with no equal. Although society and even the courts have made judgments and rulings that go against this belief, it is ultimately God and God's word which has final authority.

God is Creator and scripture states all that we are comes from God. If all that we are and all that we have are ultimately given to us by God, what does this say about anger? God created man and everything that makes us a person. When God was finished with His creation of man He said "It is good". This means that anger is good. ANGER is good! Let that sink in for a minute ... Anger IS good! Wait for it ... Anger is GOOD! Yes, anger is good; it's what we do with our anger that causes negative consequences. Our choices and behaviors are what are bad, not anger.

If anger is good—God given, then the real question is why has anger had such a negative effect in us and throughout our lives? Why have we pushed people away with our words or actions? Why do we often feel alone even when we are with a group of friends or family? Why do we hurt those we care about?

The answer is simply one word—Shame. When we are ashamed of our actions, we respond in an attempt to diminish this feeling. Anger can be responded to in several ways. See if one or more of these are familiar:

One group of people acknowledges that they are angry but then attempt to hide their anger by **suppressing** it. Since communication is 93% non-verbal, they're really only fooling themselves. Usually their body language gives it away through clenched fists or teeth, tightening of the jaw, pacing the floor, sarcasm, and so many other behaviors.

Many Christian believers have been taught to deny their anger, to turn the other cheek **repressing** their anger. This occurs when the person isn't even aware that they're angry. It is a subconscious reaction in situations where anger is triggered. Instead of acknowledging the anger, it is repressed into the depths of the soul.

Some people have been angry for so long they do not even know that they are angry from **repressing** or **suppressing** their anger. I did this in multiple ways and at various times during my life. Once I learned what I had done with my anger these methods no longer worked.

We have all witnessed and possibly even personally lost control and experienced anger explosions. This is what is commonly referred to as **aggressive** anger. This is the type of anger that leaves a wake behind it—devastating everything in its path. The scriptures teach just the opposite, *"Be angry, and sin not."* Eph. 4:26. The important distinction is being angry and addressing the action, behavior or attitude without attacking the individual.

We are all aware of people who acknowledge their anger and

use it to fuel change. They are known for getting behind causes and being **assertive** with their anger. MADD—Mothers Against Drunk Drivers impacted laws in our country. A young lady with infertility challenges wrote a devotional for 365 days of prayer for the infertile couple. A woman with a secret past abortion wrote a booklet sharing the intimate details of her choices in an attempt to help other women. A man with a past alcohol addiction leads a support group. A mother of an addict counsels and leads a support group for loved ones of addicts. A man with a sexual addiction mentors other men who share the same struggle. All of these, and so many more people, have used their anger assertively to help others.

Then there are those people who just **drop it** or choose to **deal** with their anger and move on with life. These people have a healthy understanding of what anger is and where it comes from. They also are able to put situations into perspective and determine the importance of situations.

I realized for the first time in my life I really needed more information and understanding about anger. I really needed to learn more about and attempt to understand this thing called anger.

If anger is good, for our good, or both and believing at the same time God created us, then anger would be universal. If anger is universal then why is anger more evident in some people and not as evident in all people? Some people seemingly accept their anger and use it for their benefit while others experience detriment and painful consequences which they attribute to their anger.

Anger, I learned, is an emotion. Anger is an emotion? I thought it was a feeling. I never considered the differences between feelings and emotions. Research shows that most men know or can identify six feelings falsely identifying them as emotions: Mad, Sad, Bad, Glad, Happy, and Full.

If anger is an emotion, which it is, we must then determine if it is a primary emotion (the first emotion we experience) or a secondary emotion (the second emotion we experience). This is a subtle but crucial distinction.

In order to distinguish between a primary and secondary emotion we must identify and name the very first thing we experience, and then the secondary emotion or the second thing we experience.

If anger is a primary emotion it will be the very first thing we experience. That means what we feel immediately is designed to provide protection from a threat, what is often called the fight or flight response for self-preservation. If it is a primary emotion, the first thing we experience, then we would only need to make sure our responses are appropriate for the triggering event.

If anger is a secondary emotion, a symptom or a reaction to a primary emotion being triggered, then we must measure our response to the triggering event and then ask ourselves the question if we are using our anger to deny a primary emotion or have we used anger ultimately to our own destruction.

If anger is a secondary emotion, and I am convinced it is, that means anger and its demonstration is a choice. Our anger is the result of a primary emotion Fear, Hurt/Rejection, or Anxiety not being dealt with completely or appropriately and our actions are ultimately our choice.

But someone reading right now might think, "You do not know my situation," "You don't know my wife, husband, child, boss, finances etc." You are correct; I do not know your situation.

If anger is a primary emotion, a reaction to the very first thing we experience, we would agree that we do not have a choice. But anger is a secondary emotion. Anger is a choice, a chosen response following a primary emotion being triggered.

Reactions and responses are two very different words with significantly different definitions. These words differentiate between a primary emotional reaction and a secondary emotional response. A reaction is without thought or consideration. A response is both calculated and measured.

Today in our society we do not place much emphasis on words and the weight they carry. This is one reason anger is accepted by much of society today and ultimately contributes to more anger.

In society, in our daily activities how often do we encounter people who display anger and we accept it by avoiding the issue, or just avoiding the person, or we attempt to brush it off as a momentary lapse in judgment or self-control? We often believe that when the individual's situation or circumstances change the anger will subside.

I learned that this type of rationalization is wrong. A rationalization is a little truth with a fallacy or lie woven in and through the reasoning. Anger is universal. We all experience anger but how we deal with our anger affects ourselves and our relationships differently. Some people are very aware of their anger and others are oblivious to it.

My hope is that you are investigating anger to learn about it, work through it and stop the devastating effects of unresolved anger in your life.

Question: *Do you agree you might be angry and the way you handle your anger is not working?*

Chapter 6

Lessons from the Past

The best way to evaluate the present and predict the future is to review the past. If we are to learn from our history we must look honestly at the past and learn what worked and what did not.

This is exactly what I learned when Jodi and I took the motorcycle riding and safety class. In the past I had learned to ride by trial and error and with the advice from friends. This time I was taking a course from a trained instructor. Not only has technology improved the motorcycle, it also provided insight as to what riding skills need to be learned and developed.

When we look back to the past prior to the 1900's this country was vital, growing, "necessity was the mother of invention", work ethic and commitment were the norm. Our country during this time was primarily an agricultural society transitioning into the Industrial Revolution.

A surname reflected a heritage. Love and nurturing were dominant in the home environment; honor and respect were badges of courage men desired to wear. OK, so what happened?

By observation, there are several isolated events which in their own space and time do not merit concern, but the cumulative aspect of these events over time brought with them devastation.

A little water dripping and the pool of water it forms prior to becoming a flow have little consequence but over time erosion does occur. The same can be said for our anger, over time and with accumulation destruction follows.

Consider the United States in 1913 prior to WWI. The United States was in the midst of an Industrial Revolution. Manufacturing was strong and the country was developing an infrastructure and poised for growth. WWI began and as a country remained neutral until 1917 when forced to enter the war by signed treaties with different allies. When the US entered the war the borders and lives were open to a world of influence.

The battlefield depictions are horrific and not a single American was untouched by a family member, friend, or neighbor being lost to the war. The battlefield trench warfare was in itself overwhelmingly cruel. The men would live, fight and travel in the trenches. A common war tactic was to use Mustard Gas in the trenches of the enemy combatants. The gas would immobilize the enemy and they would literally drown in their own body fluids, right there in the trenches, graves with both ends dug out. Here men would take their last stand, their last laborious breath, and here the survivors would have to crawl over their friends and comrades to escape the gas or engage the enemy in mortal battle.

Anyone today who has witnessed a person succumb to lung cancer can almost identify with the sight, the sound, and the physical pain of gas warfare. Fortunately today we have medications for pain and the ability to alleviate some of the discomfort.

When these brave survivors came home, considering the United States lost almost 90,000 men in 9 months, every home had been affected by the war. Little was spoken by these survivors of their experiences, everything within them was exhausted from trying to forget what they saw, smelled, heard, felt or witnessed.

When these men returned home from war most of them were in their 20s and 30s and many soon became husbands and fathers.

With all the killing and death these men experienced, war was not sterile and distant, their sense of self-preservation lead them to shut down emotionally. They would do most anything to never again experience the pain which in turn affected all they were emotionally and personally.

Since they themselves were at the very least guarded emotionally they were limited in what they could pass onto their heirs, what it meant to be emotionally healthy and fit.

These men in their early 20's and 30's, who in 1919 became husbands and fathers, ten years later around 1929 experienced the death of their hopes, dreams, fortunes and self-respect when the life they came to know ended on "Black Tuesday", the day the stock market crashed and the beginning of the Great Depression.

The children of the fathers who had returned from WWI are now in their early teens. This crash not only affected the people with money in the stock market, in fact the market gained composure by Friday but the damage was done, confidence was lost!

Banks closed, businesses folded and lives were totally devastated. These men who were raised in loving nurturing homes, whose fathers had passed down the desired traits of Honor, Respect and Discipline, these very recipients had experienced life at its very worst without being personally at fault. These men had been called to kill, to witness death, to witness and cause the destruction of war, and now their financial goals and dreams vanished and their hope was stripped from them. The very character traits of Respect, Honor, and Discipline which had preserved their lives in battle were now being eroded away on a daily basis.

To survive the Depression as a child of these broken men was to identify love as a meal to eat, a roof over their head and a job to provide for the necessities of life. Love in essence became a by-product of man's efforts. Men worked and pursued security through commitment to their employer, to provide for their family which also affirmed that they were providing (being loving) for their families.

It is not a coincidence that during this time the Neutrality Act 1935 was passed by Congress. The concerns of the nation were of isolationism and non-interventionism in Asia and Europe and becoming involved again in a conflict on foreign soil. This Act did not differentiate between victim or aggressor and considered both belligerent. This is a reflection of the country and the mindset of its citizens. A country of citizens, although believing in their Founding Father's ideals, merely existed and remained stagnant until the next major event—WWII.

December 7, 1941 and the attack on Pearl Harbor changed everything. This event demanded action and the United States and her citizens rose to the expectations.

Remember WWI and the men who had returned and had families? These men had witnessed such horrific experiences they had shut down emotionally therefore they could not pass on to their heir's emotional health. These heirs of WWI survivors were themselves victims, the children in their teens during the Great Depression that had learned that love was having a job, providing for your loved ones and having a roof over your head. These individuals are the men who were called upon to defend our country in WWII.

The United States went into full production to meet the war effort. Men signed up to serve in the military and the women and those men remaining took part in the war effort in manufacturing, rationing and many other ways.

These very men who left for war were already scarred and emotionally deficient and now they would experience humanity at its worst.

My father was such a man and one of the first to arrive at Dachau, a Concentration Camp. I had the unfortunate privilege to tour Dachau, an experience I will never forget. This was twenty years after my father had served in the war and was now working for the military in Germany.

Even with the passage of time, many years of maintenance and upkeep, the immaculate manicured grounds with mature foliage around the perimeter, the atmosphere was still chilling to the bone, the atrocities committed were sickening. During the camp's operation a brick building outside the camp was a shop of the camp. The shop sold lampshades made of human skin from the Jews gassed in the death chambers. My father told us that the lampshades made of human skin with tattoos was of the highest demand. A story one can never forget, questioning how can anyone experience such inhumane, barbaric actions and not be affected.

During the war, a battlefield promotion usually meant someone had been killed. The reality advancement was at the cost of another life. So many men were affected by the battle of war or the collateral destruction and death no one came through without emotional hurts, some that would never heal.

The women who sacrificed their desired roles in the home to meet the needs of the factories and war effort did so with the best of intentions. These women soon learned out of necessity to become independent and not to rely on their husbands as a provider.

Businesses realized they had another workforce from which to glean new talent and the workforce doubled. The women did offer a new dimension but at the same time wages were not growing because of the vast availability of workers.

My father often challenged the notion of independence in the home, particularly in marriage. His belief was based on his observation of the electric starter on the automobile. He believed this was the moment in history independence in marriage begun. Up until the electric starter was created in order to start an automobile it required two individuals. Women at this time were often dependent on men for transportation. While the man would crank the starter the woman would hold the button. Following the electric starter one of the two was no longer necessary.

The 1950s were a rebellious time because the youth inherently knew something was missing but could not put a name to what was lacking.

Men would go off to work and mom would be at home doing the chores. There was a dichotomy of roles in the home, the concept of waiting until the disciplinarian comes home, namely the father! This parenting technique gave fathers the proper authority and respect, but it also reinforced to the children to fear or regret their father's presence. If we are to learn to love our Heavenly Father by the example and actions of our earthly father what else could we expect than the God as the Loving, Caring, and All Sufficient Savior would be rejected by those individuals who feared or regretted their earthly father coming home.

Now society placed its faith in corporations more than churches. Theology had been usurped by science. Science had been a driving force especially during the war years but we must always remember science is merely man's observation with a hypothesis.

The 1960's were the decade of "Free Love." Love was very

much needed but the problem was the correct model to demonstrate love was broken. People began looking for love in all the wrong places—people, experiences, substances, or whatever worked. In essence, America had lost what it meant to be a family. Many homes were without fathers teaching honor, respect, and discipline, mothers reflecting loving and nurturing, and the children desiring to continue their heritage with pride.

The boys and girls of the 60's were the third generation of children raised by emotionally hurting parents. Now as parents they were unable to pass on to their children what they themselves did not have or learn.

My brother, sisters and I have had to honestly look back at family life and acknowledge how dysfunctional our family truly was. To never make an excuse for the hurts and pains of our childhood are now the "pearls" gleaned from life experiences which have made us who we are today and now offer an explanation as to what we believe and why.

1900 America an isolated society at the height of our industrial revolution.

1917 WWI

1919 Emotionally hurt men return home and start families

1929 Great Depression jobs, food, shelter are considered signs of love; children of WWI are teens

1941-1946 WWII the men and women of America are already emotionally hurting

1950 Theology is usurped by Science—man in control, Korea 1950-55 "The Forgotten War"

1960 Vietnam 1961-1975 vs. Peace & Free Love—two extremes

1970 Vietnam, Oil shortages, Iranian Hostages

1980 Lebanon/Grenada 1982-84, advancements in technology, Challenger explosion

1990 Gulf War/War on Terrorism, Communication connected with a person not a location

2000 September 11, 2001 (9/11), Natural disasters—Hurricanes Katrina, Rita, Sandy, and Harvey; political divisions

Past generations have experienced changes and growth; however, theirs were much more concrete and gradual. Today, change is immediate, often subtle, and ongoing. We have become bombarded with information, choices to be made, seldom are we able to remove ourselves and reflect upon what is happening within us. When we become numb to our emotional health, anger will prevail. Have you ever considered your family history and how history has affected your emotional health?

Chapter 7

Anger— Part of Life

Moms and dads are different for a reason. The success of having an emotionally healthy family is not the fact that there are two individuals raising a child. It is having a man and a woman raising the child.

Each and every motorcycle is unique. A motorcycle is an extension of the rider. Traditionally motorcycles were two wheels in the wind. Today we have trikes and other versions of two or three wheels. For most riders, "It doesn't matter what you ride as long as you ride." I agree although I am a traditionalist.

Both genders offer significant but different contributing factors to the upbringing of a child. In scripture men need and desire respect while women need and crave love. Respect as a primary component in males allows for a foundation for honor to be developed and rendered. Love and nurturing, the trait women pass onto their children, provide for the existence and strength of the family. When one contributing aspect or gender is missing or not in the home of the child, these crucial learnings often absorbed as if by osmosis being in proximity of the gender, the results are devastating.

The following story told by the director of a national prison ministry provides confirmation of the significance of fathers in the home. A woman, let's call her Judy, had a heart for the mothers whose sons were in prison and separated from their mothers and wives on Mother's Day. Judy's heart ached due to the fact that these women, both wives and mothers, would not receive a card on Mother's Day.

Judy took the issue upon herself and contacted a greeting card company with her concerns and offered a possible solution for both prisoners and their family members. After hearing Judy's proposal the greeting card company agreed to print Mother's Day cards for prisoners at no charge to the inmates.

The program was such a success they ran out of Mother's Day cards due to all the requests from the inmates wanting to send a card to their moms. The greeting card company, realizing the success of the program, decided to offer the same program for Father's Day. The company printed additional Father's Day cards with the anticipation of another huge success. To the amazement of everyone involved in the campaign to help the inmates remain connected with their families, not one Father's Day card was requested from any of the prisoners.

This story graphically illustrates the impact that both mothers and fathers contribute to the upbringing of their children either negatively or positively. Studies reveal a large percentage of men in prison did not have a close relationship with their fathers; many had no father in their home as a child.

With our prison population growing at alarming rates and with the divorce rate at almost 50%, America is beginning to realize from the trends how important fathers are to the makeup of the family. Men as fathers are instructed to model for their children their role as father and the associated responsibilities as defined in scriptures, presenting a strong yet compassionate balance to their children.

It would be beneficial to identify some of the different contributions that mothers and fathers do make in the lives of their children.

Some of the contributions parents provide to a child's life are basic role model examples. Some contributions have to do with what we believe God intended when he made man in His image, both male and female. Scripture depicts different roles and responsibilities for both men and women.

Earlier we examined how women are much more in touch with their feelings and emotions. We looked at how women go through a monthly menstrual cycle and how women are given the gift of carrying life in their womb. We believe that these gifts coincide with the responsibility for mothers to pass onto their children the traits of loving and nurturing.

To love in its purist form is both a learned and developed trait. In order for a person to extend love, he or she must be able to accept love himself or herself.

We must learn and understand how to accept and offer forgiveness while training ourselves to be patient with ourselves and others, how to and why we should extend grace to both others and ourselves, and how to develop the ability to look beyond a person's actions alone. Learning not to base our belief of being lovable solely on our perceptions or the actions of other people is key.

In scripture we read God called us to Love the Lord our God with all our hearts, with all our minds, with all our souls, with all our strength, **and** love our neighbor as ourselves. I read this passage of scripture regularly for years and I honestly wanted to honor God by doing as I had been commanded to do, not because I had to but because I wanted to.

I struggled for years trying to love my neighbor, trying to love and honor God. Eventually, I realized I could love God, I could truly seek Him, but I could not have love for my neighbor if I did not love myself.

This is not self-absorbent, conceit, self-centered love, ego or even id. This is referring to a love where we completely accept ourselves. We accept everything which compiles us to include our personality, weaknesses, strengths, gifts and talents. Learning to be content and accept who we are, nothing more, nothing less. When we are able to accept ourselves by choice, just as we are, this is the beginning of our ability to love our neighbor as ourselves.

The crucial question that must be answered is how much we truly love ourselves minus our accomplishments, all the things around us including family, even the trappings which identify us from degrees to job titles.

Realizing I had a love problem, it was necessary for me to see myself as God sees me. To redefine my definition of success and significance to match the definition of scripture and not the wrong definition I had learned and lived for.

Mothers are also primarily responsible for teaching us to nurture. Mothers are known for their caring maternal instincts: to hold, to stroke or caress, to comfort, to give personal attention to their loved ones, to believe in us and encourage us to become everything we are meant to be.

Loving and nurturing are so important and, without realizing it, our society is unconsciously doing away with these wonderful and necessary traits.

Mothers today, because of the pace of our lives, are now away from home more and more. Our children are in the care of others more than they are within the family. We have preschool, head start, daycare, after school programs not to mention all the sports, dance, and extracurricular activities that morph into more time away from our intended mentors, our parents.

If children do not have the quality and quantity of time with their mothers, or their mothers do not invest in them, what hope of receiving God's intended love and nurturing can we anticipate our children receiving?

What tends to happen is children learn a distorted form of love, a form of love depicted and reinforced by society as a whole. Today the concept of commitment is almost non-existent. Fidelity is rare and almost everything is based upon how I feel and what is in it for me.

Unfortunately, we see this being lived out in the percentage of young single mothers, the alarming rate of divorce, the abortion statistics, the rise in addictions, as well as the suicide rates among teens and young adults.

The change in the nurturing aspect is much harder to discern but it really became evident for me years ago. I was on an elementary school field trip with one of my boys. We were riding on a school bus when I overheard a student tell his friend that his mother had given him a pager (which today would be a cell phone) so he would know how much she loved him.

I tried to imagine in my mind, after overhearing this statement from the student, how could this child ever receive comfort from an electronic device? If this was true, that this child could know how much he was loved from a simple electronic device, then it would also be true that later in his life the more electronic boxes he accumulated the more he was loved. He would be able to have evidence that he was loved. This truly broke my heart.

All of us have observed the guilt of parents living beyond their means. We all know of parents working longer hours to meet their obligations, only later rationalizing their connectivity to their children through technology. "I may not be home but we are always in contact with one another." Nothing can replace that badly needed, frequently desired hug, eye to eye conversation and loving touch.

Fathers also contribute to their children things our society cannot and does not promote. Our society needs fathers to pass down to their children their family's unique heritage, honor, respect, and personal values.

In the past, the family surname represented a family's unique history, their contribution to society and the family significance. The Family Heritage and its contributions to society by members of its lineage, their beliefs, convictions and service by grandparents and parents are important for us to know to learn from and pass these learnings down to future generations.

Honor is a character trait that is greatly lacking in our society today. A large percentage of men do not routinely display honor for or to women anymore. How often do you witness a man standing up when a woman leaves or returns to the dinner table? Men seldom show honor to one another. When do we observe younger men deferring to their elders in public? Men of scripture demonstrated and passed down their faith and values to their families. When have you attended a church service when there were more men than women and children in attendance?

Men not demonstrating honor towards women as in the past by their conduct was likely brought about by the women's liberation movement and political correctness. Men supporting and agreeing with the precepts of the women's movement that women have equal value to men often did not want to offend women. Women desiring to be seen as equals denied their softer feminine qualities.

A man is designed to have someone to provide and care for, to protect and share a future with. In scripture the relationship between husbands and wives is often used as a comparison of the church, the Bride of Christ. The church is the Bride of Christ for whom God gave his Son, Jesus to die, so that His church may live.

Husbands should do no less for their wives. In fact, that is exactly what husbands are called to do. Men need to honor women in the way they look at a woman. When a man has a daughter the decision to look at women the way he wants men to look at his precious daughter is an easy one to make. Men need to honor women in the way they interact with women on a daily basis understanding their difference with different needs and perceptions acknowledging these differences and learn how to act appropriately.

Fathers should pass on to their children the trait of respect. Respect for faith in God, respect for self, respect for others. This is a trait that must be learned, experienced, personally owned and regularity passed on to others. Respect for God is much more than going to church or holding to a moral code or being a good person. This trait of respect is only accomplished through a relationship based on a foundation of honesty and truth that is alive, always growing, always going deeper, ever challenging but always based on the character of God, not a feeling or emotion.

Respect for self is for many the hardest trait to personally own. This trait is developed by owning and learning from our past experiences never excusing our choices. Taking complete ownership of the decisions we made and the consequences we endured following our decisions. These learnings and the insights we gained from our past when we reflect and honestly evaluate ourselves never comparing ourselves to anyone else is when we begin to have self-respect.

Those of us that did not have a mother in our lives, or our mother was unable to nurture or teach us our personal value, must learn about our personality and all that we are from a true and accurate accounting.

Mothers often have the greatest influence on us while we are infants and toddlers; as we progress through childhood towards maturity our fathers seal our training. A child desires to know that they have value and they are accepted even when they fail—missing the last pitch in a baseball game or when not chosen for the dance team.

Respect for self is accepting ourselves even when we are not the best, the first, or even correct. If a parent is always asking for more, for a better performance the false perception that could be communicated to the child is my value is contingent on self-accomplishment, performance and perfection. When a child believes their value is based on approval and they do not receive what has been reinforced anger will develop.

Spend time at any youth sports activity and observe this reality. Look particularly for the fathers; observe their body language and facial expressions. You will see different reactions to their child's performance. If you observe the children you will then see the effects. You will see some children that believe they cannot meet the expectations set for them by others but, hopefully you will also see those children that although they may not be stars they have confidence and self-respect.

Our focus on performance or good behavior and accomplishments can be as extreme as the difference between punishment and discipline.

Punishment often is the result of being emotionally charged and is intended to inflict pain or break our will. Discipline is intended to change or modify an attitude. Notice the word choice of changing an attitude instead of behavior. We often focus solely on behavior and then the attitude does not change or even follow the desired behavior. Focusing on a person's attitude the behavior will naturally follow.

Focusing on behavior and not attitude can be learned from the situation of a little strong-willed girl (we will call her Ann) and her mother. Mom tells Ann to sit down, Ann says no. Mom tells Ann to sit down and Ann still ignores her mom. Mom continues to repeatedly tell Ann to sit down to no avail. Finally mom gets up and forces Ann into a sitting position. Now the question to be answered is this, Is Ann sitting down on the outside or the inside? Without question Ann is sitting down on the outside, but inside Ann is standing proud and developing a lifelong behavior pattern. Too often we focus solely on behavior because that is what we see, it is easier to measure and monitor, and it also provides us with immediate gratification for our need to be respected.

If we would only take the time to dig a little deeper to identify the attitudes that need to be addressed in our children and ourselves, we would experience greater success in changing bad behaviors and reap the benefit from the lasting rewards.

A few disciplines a father passes on to his children are the ability to maintain control in the midst of chaos, consider others regarding the use of our words and our actions, and to complete the tasks that need to be completed even when we do not enjoy doing them or when we never receive recognition for doing them

Unfortunately, society and many individuals have conformed to the immediate gratification, quick fix, just in time, just enough, just to get by mentality. Many today no longer desire to commit the time and energy required before experiencing the desired results.

Think about the contrast of a farmer and a consumer. The consumer passes the fields on the way to the grocery store to purchase his daily meals. The consumer does not know the effort needed to plant the crop in advance of the harvest or the hard work necessary to prepare the soil for the greatest chance of a successful crop. Not to mention the long hours of the planting process and the stress of continual maintenance and care. The daily concerns about the effects of the weather or pests. All of this a farmer endures even before the first evidence of any measure of success. The time, energy, commitment, and sacrifices by the farmer necessary to bring to the grocery market goods for others to consume.

The concept of obedience before blessings is also missing in our society. The very idea of "being still" is foreign to most of us. The scriptures promote this value in Psalm 46: "Be Still and Know I am God." To be still is a learned and developed discipline. This discipline can be also applied to our tongue, our behavior and our anger.

Earlier we learned that we will not be without anger so we must learn to express anger appropriately. This requires self-discipline in conjunction with Respect, Honor and Love, and with the right attitude we will be able to be angry—sin not.

A question to consider is how are Honor, Respect, and Love being demonstrated in your life?

Chapter 8

Getting Back on Course

In basic navigation to determine if on course we must first determine where we are. We begin with where we were when we began in relation to where we are currently relative to our intended destination. My brother, an Airborne Ranger, would tell me, "Tim, I am never lost, just temporarily disoriented."

This is often the case when riding motorcycles. You find yourself riding and suddenly you are taking a turn to explore a new route or to check out what is around the bend or over the hill.

In the past when airplanes were actually controlled by pilots and not computers, more than 90% of a pilot's time and energy was spent on getting the plane back on course.

Many of us believe we start at point A and then fly a straight course to point B. The problem with this thought is there are so many naturally occurring events and conditions that affect flight; winds, storms, temperature changes and even faulty readings; therefore it is necessary to continually monitor your course of flight always diligent to maintain your course of heading for your intended point of destination.

Getting back on course in our lives isn't always easy, but it isn't impossible either. It requires a lot of hard work. The hard work of digging through our life experiences, the sequences of events, in our lives. Identifying and learning about our feelings and emotions, what our motives were when we made the decisions and choices of our past and the true intentions that drive us. Once we are on course for our final desired intended destination all our efforts and the pain we will endure will be considered worthwhile.

Man has always had a problem with maintaining a course for life. In the Old Testament book of Deuteronomy, the last book of the Jewish Torah, Moses had gone to Mt. Sinai and God had spoken directly to the people. Not to their fathers, but to the people. God gave the people laws by which to live to achieve success according to Him. Unfortunately, the people to whom God personally spoke soon forgot about Him and neglected to honor Him. This is not much different from those of us today.

The Lord so desired His people to honor Him but the people chose to do as they saw fit. They believed they knew a better way—their way. His chosen people tried to live a righteous life but it was never good enough in their eyes, and in turn they attempted to appease their failings by seeking other gods, but with no success.

When Moses came down from the mountain top after meeting with God he held two stone tablets which God had given to him with His laws written upon them by God.

When Moses realized how quickly the people had turned from God, Moses threw down the tablets to the ground smashing them. This was a reflection of what the people had done to the Love of God.

For many of us this unfortunately is a great analogy of our lives and the poor choices we have made. God created us and said, "It is good," but we did not believe or accept this truth. In our own ways we have taken our lives and smashed them to pieces.

It is now necessary for us to chisel away all that does not reflect what God intended for our lives to reflect. Later in the Book of Deuteronomy, Moses was instructed by God to chisel out two tablets and bring them before God and God once again wrote His law upon them.

We should not believe it to be a coincidence that God gave us His laws on tablets of stone. Jesus our Lord, Savior and Cornerstone of the Christian faith was believed to be born in a cave, a void in rock, then lay in a manger. Joseph, the father of Jesus, was most likely a stone craftsman not a carpenter of wood. Jesus was buried in a tomb, an open section of rock which could not contain him. We are instructed through the scriptures that our lives were intended to be examples of what God has done and often we have stone markers upon our graves, standing stones representing our lives.

A question to reflect upon is what in your life do you need to chisel away to be more at peace with yourself and others? This is an imperative step towards intimacy with another person because we must know ourselves before we are able to be completely open and vulnerable to another.

To truly know who we are we must first know from where we come. Here is a glimpse into my life as I share some of my life experiences. I believe sharing what I have learned from my past will help you dig deeper into your own history to learn and better understand from where your anger originates.

My father was born in 1918, a WWI war baby, my mother was born in 1921. These two dates are significant because these dates had everything to do with my parents' schema, the two people from whom I learned the most over the course of my life.

My father was born the year the U.S. entered WWI. America

lost 90,000 lives in 9 months of war, not a single family in America was left un-scared. My parents, born when they were, were raised by those with scars from the Great War, lived through the depression, later experienced the trauma of WWII while serving and being members of "The Greatest Generation," then entered into the "new generation" as parents of two generations of children over a 13 year period.

I tell people I was the only child in a family of six even though I had three siblings. The reason for me saying this is because one sister is nine years older, my brother ten years, and my oldest sister twelve years my senior. In essence, I was raised as an only child—this will have an influence explained later. My mother was in her forties when I was born and this was not as normal then as it is today so frequently my parents were perceived as grandparents by friends. I was definitely unexpected and always told I was a surprise.

My mother had a drinking problem during most of her life. My brother told me stories of times he witnessed our father pouring out bottles of alcohol into the toilet. Our parents drank, often to excess, realizing later in life that my father drank to escape the rantings of our mother.

My father often worked several jobs to make ends meet before finally gaining employment with the United States Government as a Department of the Army Civilian in the Comptroller's Division of the Army. This offered our family a life full of adventures and experiences few people would ever know. My father's position provided him with the opportunity to realize his dream of giving his family the world through travel.

Our world of travel began in 1962 when I was only three years old. We moved from the New Jersey shore to Sierra Vista, Arizona in the middle of the Southwestern Desert two and a half hours from a community of any size. We lived in Sierra Vista and shortly thereafter moved to Tucson, and approximately a year later moved again, this time to Orleans, France just outside Paris.

The year was 1965 and in a three year span of time our family left the comfort of the American way of life of the East Coast of the United States, lived in the desert of Arizona and then moved to Orleans, France. We were now living in France, a culture unlike our own, where we didn't speak the language and were strangers in a foreign land.

Our family lived for three months in a hotel room until finding an apartment in the city of Orleans. I tell about my play time following the maids around the hotel during their daily routine of cleaning rooms, including bathrooms. To this day I despise cleaning toilets. Our family would travel by bus to the American Military Concern where immediately upon arrival, as we passed through the gate, we were greeted by a military police soldier and felt safe and secure. After a few short hours we would once again leave from the comfort of the American way of life on the American Concern and return to our apartment in downtown Orleans, France.

Our family lived in France until the French Government expelled the American Force and my father was transferred to Germany. We then lived in a nearby small German community until moving into an apartment on the Army Post. In 1970, we finally returned to the United States.

Opportunities while in Europe were fabulous for me living thirty minutes outside of Paris and later living in Germany! I can say I have viewed Paris from the top of the Eiffel Tower, the Arch De' Triumph, visited Versailles and the Louvre. I have strolled the Champs De Elise', toured southern France including the Loire Valley home of some of the finest wines of the world.

While living in Germany I was fortunate to travel to Berlin, the Black Forest, and Munich. Our mother and father saw that they made the most of our time in Europe, also traveled to Austria, Switzerland, Denmark, Copenhagen, Brussels, and England. We crossed the English Channel and saw the Cliffs of Dover, a memory of our father from WWII, later returned to the US crossing the Atlantic Ocean on the last running of the USS United States.

Having lived outside the United States for almost half my life, then returning to my country of birth, seeing the Statue of Liberty on Ellis Island and the American Flag in New York Harbor, I have a great appreciation and love of my county.

My childhood was filled with events and experiences that were fantastic, but I also experienced isolation from family and the people with whom I could bond and develop lifelong relationships. Moving was always in my future as I attended thirteen schools in just twelve years. Different countries brought about different languages, customs and cultures not to mention the many changes of friends. However, the feelings of fear, hurt, rejection, and anxiety began to develop, layering one on top of the other, emotions I was unable to identify or deal with.

While overseas my eldest sister married in 1966 and left home, my brother left to attend college in the states in 1967, and my other sister left for college in the states the following year leaving me alone with our parents in a foreign country being raised as an only child and feeling disconnected from my siblings.

My mother was deeply isolated, feeling alone and longing for the connection with others yet her alcohol problem only pushed her friends and us away by her hurtful words. Our family weathered the storms of life coming through them stronger but not without hurts which today are only scars. Scars tell where we have been, not what we have become.

My parents and I returned home from Europe in 1970 only to move again my freshman year in 1973, this time to Panama, South America, home of the Panama Canal Zone.

This move also had its wonderful and beneficial experiences, but it too came with different loses. Our first month there, while my parents were sleeping in our new apartment and I was at a friend's house, my parents were drugged and robbed. This prompted a constant concern for safety which was later reinforced by a young soldier being brutally beaten by the local police for having 2 aspirin in his pocket, which they claimed to be contraband. Later we lived on an Army Post not twenty yards from the jungle having a three toed sloth, a black panther that had killed small household pets, and deadly snakes in the back yard. Even the toads there were deadly to pets.

This was a time in my youth when I needed to experience as many opportunities as possible through extracurricular activities and school functions, however my limitations were the limited transportation options to and from these activities as well as concern for my parents drinking and driving. It was necessary for us to travel through the Republic of Panama to and from my school. Conditions were not always safe nor did we want to give the police a reason to detain us. There were even two occasions during this time when all American personnel were called to remain on post for a period of time due to political uprisings in the local community.

Here I was living in one of the most amazing places in the world, in the midst of the jungle with one of the greatest engineering accomplishments of all time—the Panama Canal. Living in a state of intrigue coupled with fear. The dichotomy of emotions were difficult to understand, always present, never identified.

These are some of the major experiences in my life but there were smaller ones that came to mind when I dug into my past.

My home environment, the makeup of our family, changed while living in Europe following my sister leaving home for marriage, my brother's departure, and later my other sister leaving for college. During this time our mother experienced losses which brought out her anger and in our father's need for self-preservation he disconnected emotionally from family. My father was always physically present with us but he was emotionally removed. This was the time in life I needed a father the most, and my father was unavailable—another layer of rejection.

I also had physical limitations which reinforced my perception of being less than complete. My eyesight was a challenge ever since I was a child. Crooked and crowded teeth left me feeling self-conscious and embarrassed, my smiles were controlled. A torn ligament in my knee about age ten which never completely healed was always a concern. I have always been aware of my flaws from poor vision to crooked teeth to limitations with my knee which reinforced what I thought I was "damaged goods." These issues provided one more layer of insecurities, anxiety and fear of rejection.

However, I remember the first time wearing glasses as a high school student living in Panama, how for the first time I could see the vines of the jungle, individual leaves on the trees not just the mass of green I had come to know. I began to see with clarity, not just literally but figuratively. Later in my twenties, I got braces on my teeth and I was finally willing to openly smile. The first time in my life open to myself and others, as much as I was able.

I realized I began believing less of myself from a childhood experience when I was about five years old. I had been attending a vacation bible school and I remember being in a doctor's office for a check-up and proudly telling the doctor "I promise to wash my feet every day." *I had connected the soles of my feet with my person, my feet being dirty and my soul in need to be clean.* Isaiah 5:18 NLT

These personal experiences, false beliefs, perceptions and observations were informative of how I related with each of my parents at different times during my life. My dad and I had a close relationship until I was about eight, not really remembering a connection with my mother during that time, although I was close with my sister during those years. I do not remember being connected with my father from my teens until I was almost twenty. During this time my mom and I had a close relationship but it changed drastically when I entered college. During the years disconnected from my dad I connected with my mom. Fortunately, I reconnected with him in my twenties and we remained close the rest of my dad's life. This constant change in connection with my parents became a negative pattern for connections later in life.

Can you identify with any of my story? What were your family dynamics during your formative years, the foundation on which our lives are built upon? Only later in life did my sister and I, through conversations, begin to realize the dysfunction of our family. Everything on the exterior looked "normal," the family made sure, which is very common in families with addiction issues. When asked about my life I always portrayed a life to be desired by others, the experiences of a lifetime, the benefits few in the world would ever have while at the same time minimizing the sacrifices and losses that came as a result. How truly wonderful and rewarding are our memories and experiences. If they are too good to be true—they probably are.

Psalm 107—Doing the work of digging.

Are you willing to do the hard work necessary to find peace? It is crucial to learn from our past which is the foundation on which we build our future lives. A thorough understanding of how and why we relate to others can come from looking back at our past experiences, acknowledging the influence they have made, while having the fortitude to break free of them. This reflective learning is to provide an explanation, never an excuse, for the choices we make.

Chapter 9

Masks

Motorcycle riders often have discussions regarding helmets. Some states require helmets, some do not. Motorcycle helmets come in various versions, designs and colors. Motorcyclists can chose from full face versions, open face helmets, to skull caps or brain buckets. The full face version offers the greatest protection by encompassing the rider's head and face. Helmets with a face shield protect the rider from the elements. Wearing either helmet is similar to wearing a mask. I always wear a helmet because a helmet also offers protection from the wind, road debris. Being older I am not able to dodge the bugs as I once was. Bugs hurt!

As a husband and father struggling with personal and family issues, I found myself running almost every day at a soccer complex near our home. I ran during my college years because I enjoyed it. On this day I ran because I needed to run. This is a metaphor for my life. I was running not because I enjoyed running. I was running from life, from myself.

I remember running in the desert of Arizona in the early mornings, hearing the coyotes howl as if to call to one another saying, "Here comes breakfast." I also remember running in West Virginia at the beginning of a snow storm. The vivid contrast of black asphalt with white snow as it began to stick and accumulate on the surface. The sensation of the chill in the air as it entered my body with each breath, the perspiration on my skin due to the heat generated by my exertion of energy, the cold air on my face as the temperature was dropping. These were times when running was pure pleasure. Now I found myself running to find joy, to find peace, to escape pain.

What a contrast between the reasons to run. When I would leave the house for a run my children would ask, "How long will you be gone?"

My standard answer was "When I am finished."

One day as I was walking out the door, before it was completely closed, I overheard my daughter say to her siblings, "Dad will be home when he has worked through his issues."

Wow—what insight from my daughter. Her insight was both accurate and troubling at the same time. My daughter was able to see what I could not see; she could see beneath my Mask, she could see what I was trying to cover and hide from, to dismiss.

Running had become a mask, self-medication, a way of numbing my hurts and feelings of rejection, the nonphysical emotion of hurt in my life. Often we will become involved in activities in an attempt to take care of ourselves, gain acceptance, fill our resume, and/or help others. These are good things, but when done to cover up our hidden pain they ultimately leave us empty. We can do the right things for the wrong reasons.

With the mask removed (running), realizing my daughter had named it, the mask no longer worked. I was naked and vulnerable. I could attempt to find another mask, another way to hide from hurt, but I realized a mask would never work again. I would always know if I was wearing a mask. Once we identify what compels us to do something, that activity no longer medicates the pain or meets our hidden need.

This is what often happens in addiction. At first just a little of something and they have an experience. Then it takes a little more just to meet the level of their first time experience. Then even a whole lot more will not take them back to the first time experience level so they try something new. Addicts are addicted to re-experiencing their first time high.

Running, my addiction, was considered good so I could proudly tell friends and others how often and even how far I ran. Soon running became a moniker, a badge of honor. In our exercise enthralled society running was accepted and even applauded.

What I came to realize was running, while exhilarating, was actually numbing my pain. The more I ran the more I pushed away the deep-seated emotions of fear, hurt, rejection, and anxiety.

Then I began to look for what other masks I was wearing or had worn to self-medicate. I found titles: Senior Technical Sales Representative, Vice-President of a Charter School, Church Leader, Lay Pastor/Counselor, and District Training Chairman. These positions with their titles were good and worthy endeavors, but as I began to look beneath my masks I asked myself, why did I hold the position? Was I truly committed to the organization or was I using the organization as a means for personal fulfillment?

I also had to ask questions regarding relationships and friendships. Were my friendships with leaders and experts in my profession based on friendship or for selfish ambition? Did I need identification with experts and leaders? Was I pursuing relationships with others who were in more dysfunctional situations so I could feel better about myself? What things had I acquired to minimize pain, what material possessions did I use to negate or diminish loses? These are hard and embarrassing questions to ask. The answers are often troubling, as well as revealing. I have heard it said, "Confession may not be good for our reputation, but it is great for the soul."

Sometimes we find ourselves chasing after new adventures, new places to explore where no one knows us and we do not have to experience past memories. We schedule activities in our lives so we never have to be still and have the time to think about our pain or deal with our past. These are all masks I used at one time or another to self-medicate as an escape from emotional pain. The problem is once we identify a Mask it is no longer a mask but a means to hide. What Masks are you wearing? What are you hiding from? What emotions are you avoiding? Are you ready and willing to remove your mask so you can honestly see yourself and one day allow another to see you as you truly are? Intimacy = In-to-me-see.

Chapter 10

The Great Commandment

Love the Lord your God with all your heart and with all your mind. This is the first and greatest commandment. And the second is like it, Love your neighbor as yourself. All the law of the prophets hang on this.   Matthew 22:37-39

Love the Lord your God. Many of us have done this our entire lives. We truly do love God with everything we have. We love God because He is God. We love God because He is Holy. We love God because He is worthy. We love God because He loved us first. Most of us who profess to love God do love God, we truly do love Him with everything we have.

Understanding that we experience primary and secondary emotions, pure love, the love God intended, requires the absence of Fear, Hurt/Rejection and Anxiety. When we have not completely addressed and worked through these primary emotions we will be charged with anger. This is why I believe we must deal with anger not just manage it. Managing our anger requires us to focus on our anger which limits our ability to love. When we deal with our anger we acknowledge where it came from and resolve it so we are able to love unselfishly.

The commandment to love God is not what we personally struggle with. What we struggle with is the conjunction word **and**! Yes, that little word we use every day, the word following the commandment to Love God, **and** the second is ... as yourself.

How much do I love myself? Is this a question you've ever thought of? I asked this very question of myself and I did not like the answer, the honest answer.

I asked myself the question, on a scale of 1 to 10, with 1 being the least and 10 being the most, how much do you love yourself? My answer was 3. Yes, a 3. I loved myself as a 3 out of a possible 10. That was a hit in the gut, it broke my heart. I then went back to scripture and thought how much do I love God? I loved God with everything I had, but everything I had was a 3 out of a possible 10. I loved God with my all. The underlying question was how much was my all?

Believing the scriptures are the Word of God, if we love ourselves as a 3 and we are commanded to Love our neighbor as ourselves, we are only able to love our neighbor at the very most as a 3. Let that sink in. If you only love yourself as a 3, as I had, all you can love others is a 3.

The next question we must ask is, who is our neighbor? Our neighbor can be anyone with whom we have an awareness, acquaintance, or personal relationship.

Consider this: If our wife loves us as a 10, but we only love ourselves as a 3, how much of her love can we receive? The answer has to be 3. We can only receive the love of a 3. The reverse is also true. We may love her with all we have, but it is still only a 3. If she loves us as a 10 there will be a void which may explain why she doesn't feel loved.

God loves us so much that He Gave His Son so that we might

live. See, God loves us His measure of 10. How much of His love can we receive if we only love ourselves as a 3? The answer must be 3.

Realizing my anger resulted from not dealing with my primary emotions and my ability to love was limited, I began to consider the difference between like and love. Love being a command, like being a choice.

As a parent of teenagers at the time, I re-framed the question. I was able to ask the kids in their church youth group: "How many of you believe your parents love you?"

More than 95% of the kids said their parents love them. They justified their answer of being loved because they were in fact their parent's children, or because their parents were Christian people or just because they were supposed to.

I then asked: "How many of your parents like you?"

Less than 20% of the kids said they believed their parents liked them. Love and Like—what is the difference? The difference is we are called to love which we often do out of obligation, not by choice while liking is about a desire, a choice we make. The differences between these two words and their definitions require us to ask the following questions:

1. *Do I love God out of obligation or desire?*

2. *Do I try to love myself out of obligation or desire?*

3. *Do I try to love my neighbor out of obligation or desire?*

4. *Do I like God?*

5. *Do I like me?*

6. *Do I like my neighbor?*

God is big enough to handle these questions and the honesty of our answers. Questions allow us to grow personally and then if we answer them honestly our relationships will benefit.

God is described as a Lion and Lamb, two animals representing very different ends of the spectrum within the animal kingdom. The Lion: King of the Jungle, powerful, fearful, dominating, growling, distant, intimidating, devouring. The Lamb: gentle, soft, passive, warm, playful, cuddly, safe. These two animals are used as metaphors for God. When you think of God, which animal is the first image that comes to your mind?

For many the very first image of God is a Lion. The distant and dominating, intimidating King. Our perception of God has a direct correlation to how and why we worship and serve Him. If we perceive God as a Lion we will most likely serve and worship Him more out of fear, judgment and obligation than love. On the other hand, if our first image of God is that of a Lamb we may forget His authority, our position relative to His, the reverence, worship and awe He deserves and expects. Scriptures use both animals as a symbol yet neither is exclusive; it is a perfect blend of the two.

One of the most inspiring and challenging passages is in the book of Revelation, chapter 5. The author's imagery of the multitudes of people before the throne, so many people they were unable to be counted due to the very number present, then absolute silence. This visual brings chills to many. Can you imagine being in the very presence of God, multitudes worshiping Him, giving him praise and then an Angel puts a finger close to his lips and says shush and then ... total silence?

When you first think of God do you see him as a Lion or do you see him as a Lamb? Both are possible. How you identify God will have a direct reflection on how you serve and why you honor Him. Our perception of God also will influence how we interpret the Scriptures and present the cross to others. If we see God as a lion we will gravitate towards condemnation of others unlike ourselves, those we perceive as less than deserving. If we see Christ as a Lamb we might have the tendency to provide abounding worldly grace, political correctness, ensuring not to offend anyone. We must have harmony in both truth and grace to present the cross as scripture dictates.

Our perception of God will also influence how we see and relate to others; the people we love, the people we encounter on a daily basis. Often the way we relate to God or even with others is out of fear which limits our ability to be truthful and open; although we will rarely admit this to ourselves or others. This can be a fear we do not measure up to or the basic fear of rejection.

One night while my son and I were just hanging out he asked me about fear. We were talking and he asked, "Isn't fear the absence of control?" From the mouth of babes truth is spoken. Fear is the lack of control! If we are brutally honest with ourselves we really do not control anything. We may think we do and even try to convince ourselves we are in control, but ultimately we do not control much of anything.

We are called in scripture to fear God which is not a common or popular teaching in churches today. This was much more common in the Christian Church of the past which we can confirm by looking at past sermons. Teaching to Fear God is not as popular today because most everything in our society is about feeling good, all about me, and what we believe we are able to control.

If fear is the loss of control and we are called to fear God, then we are actually called to relinquish control to God. This being truth and if our definition of God is correct we honestly do not relinquish anything to Him. Everything is His; it is only a paradigm shift in our system of beliefs when we willingly give control to God.

To fear God is to Give God control—what peace this truly provides to those willing to Honor and Worship their God.

Control—what do you think you actually control? I found out I do not control anything but myself. Even that is limited because there are things in me that are out of my control. My endocrine system or my heart beating is out of my control. Realizing I did not really control as much as I thought, I willingly gave up trying to control most things in my life. By giving up control, I ultimately gave up power. I had been taught, and society reinforces the idea, power is control. I had used anger as a means of power, which was ultimately, a desire for control.

When this transformation occurred, the thrill of the hunt, the closing of the sale and anticipated wins had little rewards because I had been doing things for the wrong reason. I had been doing these things and seeking accomplishments to compensate for my insecurities. Not for the purest of reasons of helping others and making a positive contribution to society.

1. *What do you believe you control?*

2. *How much control must you have?*

When we learn about fear and control we begin to realize how much of life is about a desire to be in control and we mistakenly believe when we're in control we can "control" the outcomes of life. This is not a control problem as much as it is a God problem. This is a God problem because we have placed ourselves into a position of being God.

Life is a process and once we are convinced the process will continue in some form from birth to eternity without our directing everything we become free. We can debate the concept of eternity but in the end it all comes down to what we know, or don't know. We only know what we know; we don't know what we don't know.

Learning this is humbling to say the least. When we acknowledge we are not God we become realistic of our position and limitations. When we attempt to be in control of everything in life while falsely believing we control the outcomes, we are seeking perfection. Seeking perfection as we perceive it to be, we are the ones setting a standard to be met. By setting the standard we are making ourselves God. Again, we have a God problem.

The pursuit of perfection or control is ultimately based on personal performance. This method to achieve control by perfect performance is defeating especially over time. If we attempt perfection and do not achieve it in our minds we are now failures. If we do achieve the perceived standard of perfection which we have established for ourselves and we do not maintain that level of performance or accomplishment we are now a failure. Either way we fail.

For my entire life I have pursued perfection. I was your classic perfectionist being told by people in my life who were the closest to me, "You are your worst critic." I now realize my desire for perfection was born out of anger.

Never understanding how much I valued perfection until I began losing relationships with people I valued most. I never thought twice about unconsciously holding someone to a standard of performance or expectation. I did not think it was wrong because I was not holding anyone to the standard I had set for myself—perfection.

My standard for my performance was perfection. I held others to a standard below mine.

> ### Tim = Perfection
> ---
> <u>others</u>   <u>others</u>
> <u>others</u>

Reasoning that my level of performance was perfection and superior to the level I had set for others I believed I was not wrong. It was wrong because I had set a level of performance for myself and others. A standard I would never achieve causing constant frustration. Setting a standard for someone else—even if it is our own perception is wrong because in essence I made myself God. By setting standards of personal performance, I had a God problem. I had allowed trials, situations and circumstances in life to become bigger than God. Realizing what I had done, how my life had been lived, I needed to repent, to change my ways, and seek forgiveness and offer forgiveness to and from others. Setting standards and desiring perfection is honorable but not always realistic. I have since learned, "Better is the enemy of good, perfection the enemy of best."

We need to train ourselves to accept others just as they are. This requires gentleness. Having the desire to be gentle requires us to train ourselves to respond out of grace. We must not see or love others based on our standard or expectation. We must never allow our shortcomings, strengths, limitations, talents, or a need for others to like us to dictate our relationships.

True gentleness given by a strong individual is much more appreciated, valued and real than gentleness without strength. Many men today, especially the more masculine male, have a difficult time if not a complete lack of desire or ability to identify with the men of scriptures that society has emasculated.

Reading the scriptures we observe males represented as strong, rough, raw male figures with dirt between their toes, calloused hands, and the willingness to stand for what they believed.

Society has changed this true representation of what it means to be a male out of a need for political correctness. A true male can hold a hurting woman providing comfort while being a safe place for her to fall. A man can embrace a baby, a child or a small creature with gentleness and compassion while fighting the battle. This is what we as males are called to do. Being such a male is true gentleness through strength.

But when Christ had offered for all time a single sacrifice for sins, he sat down at the right hand of God, waiting from that time until his enemies should be made a footstool for his feet.

For by a single offering he has perfected for all time those who are being sanctified. Hebrews 10:10-14

It is necessary to have a correct definition of perfection. Our definition cannot be of man, it must be of God. In this scripture, it states, *"For by a single offering he has perfected ..."* which means He has made us complete in Him through Christ. This is one of the most freeing and life changing convictions we can ever have. Our perfection, being complete, comes from what God has done. We have done nothing to be seen by Him as perfect. It was by the sacrifice of His Son that we are made perfect, we are complete.

Can you imagine how this would change our self-image if we really believed and owned this verse? How many young girls and women would be at peace with their looks? How many boys and men would see themselves completely different?

The visual of Jesus sitting at the right hand of God has such significance we cannot ignore or fail to understand its importance. In biblical times and the times of kings the left hand signified guilt while the right hand signified innocence. When an accused person was brought before the King he knew before the verdict was given whether he was found innocent or guilty depending in which hand the verdict was held. Jesus is sitting at the right hand of God the Father, which without another word determines our innocence. How do you see yourself differently after reading and believing this truth of Jesus sitting at the right hand of God?

What does the reference to Holy mean? This verse tells us that we are not only perfect but we are in the "Process of being made Holy." Holy means that by the death of Jesus, the Son of God, we are being set apart and one day we will be without sin or blemish and in the presence of our Holy God totally complete and set apart.

When we own and internalize this verse our faith, world, and ability to love will be changed forever. When we realize we have gotten it all wrong all these years regarding love, admitting our definition of love was based more on the performance of love through demonstration by ourselves and others than for love itself, we became lovable with the pure desire and ability to love.

Because of my compensation ambitions and masks, when I was angry most people would never believe how little love I had for myself. Unfortunately many people today, especially "church people," believe the problem with society today isn't that people lack love for themselves; it is that they love themselves too much. When asked why they believe this they often give a list of things people do that may be perceived as selfish and loving oneself. In my experiences relating with people in diverse communities; churches, veterans, motorcyclists, businesses, a large number of the people do not believe they are loved or lovable, although their outward persona exudes confidence and self-love.

The appearance of self-love through things or actions is a symptom of a deeper problem, a problem that things and actions can never compensate for. Their behaviors are compensation ambitions or proven ways to provide an anticipated result to feel better, to feel good, to feel loved. True love, as God intended, comes from us learning to love ourselves as He loves us, believing we are complete and perfect. Out of this love, we can love our neighbors as ourselves.

On a scale of 1—10, how much do you love yourself?

Chapter 11
Self-Esteem ... Not!

Does the motorcycle fit the rider? This is the question to ask, not "Does this motorcycle make me look young and cool?" Often people struggling with their identity will compensate in ways we never consider; urban residents driving a big truck never using the truck for its designed purpose, middle aged men buying the biggest and most powerful motorcycle available. When self-esteem dictates personal worth, outward appearances are of primary importance. Self-respect requires nothing more.

For years, our society has been consumed with an individual's self-esteem. We see this displayed in our schools doing away with failing grades, some even doing away with grades altogether, and now it is about attendance and participation. Teachers are encouraged not to use red ink when grading papers because of the negative connotations with corrections in red.

The focus on self-esteem at the expense of reality is not limited to our schools. We see this in some recreational sports programs doing away with keeping score. The "loser's" self-esteem may be negatively affected so they don't keep score or declare any team a winner.

We see this being reinforced in television sitcoms and in the real-life drama shows by avoiding telling the participants they do not meet the expectations. It is amazing how many participants believe they are the next idol or super star, believing they are exceptionally gifted because so many people in their lives never speak truth to them out of the fear of hurting their feelings or being rejected by them. When these contestants come face to face with an objective opinion (reality) it is often devastating for them and they cannot reconcile why they were not chosen to compete.

How many times have we heard people say, or maybe we have said to someone we desire to encourage, "You can be anything you want to be." When we say this, are we being completely honest and setting the very person we care for up for failure? Really wanting to be a major league baseball player does not guarantee we will make the cut, be drafted making the team. It really does matter if we're not able to see the ball as it leaves the pitcher's hand, or run fast enough, or are strong enough to hit the ball out of the park. These talents, abilities, and physical conditions do matter and are necessary to become a major leaguer. When we choose not to speak truth to those we care about out of fear of hurting their self-esteem (feelings), ultimately we are doing them more harm than good. We must be honest while at the same time providing encouragement. We can encourage them to pursue a career in baseball, just not as a player.

The difference between hurt and harm is that harm is for a longer duration. This is why doctors take the oath "To do no harm." Doctors do not take an oath to not cause pain. Pain is often a necessary experience in order to bring about healing.

If we reverse the word order of Self-Esteem to Esteem-Self we get a much more accurate explanation of our motives. We are not concerned about truth or being correct or right, we are more concerned about self, Esteeming-Self. Not only is this wrong, it is limiting. This defines our value as being limited to what we achieve or acquire. If our career is recognized as successful then we are therefore a success—we have value. If the things we have acquired are valuable to society then we hold value. If our relationships are fulfilling and intact, then we have value and these things, along with our other accomplishments we have acquired, have worth and we are to be valued.

Understanding these limitations, conditions and fallacies of Self-esteem makes us wonder what other choice we have. The other option is acquiring Christ-esteem which is esteeming Christ. Putting Him first, giving Him praise, and worshiping Him for all that we are because of what He has done.

Self-Esteem   **Christ-Esteem**

"Esteeming Self"   **"Esteeming Christ"**

With the same applications we see that "self" is limited to what value we can possible achieve; whereas in Christ our value is without measure. We can rest in the fact that our value is not determined by our past, present or even our future. Our value was determined in the past by the Cross before we were even conceived. What an amazing reality providing relief and peace.

How do we transition from living through self-esteem to living in Christ-Esteem. The answer is Salvation, believing and trusting in the Lord your God.

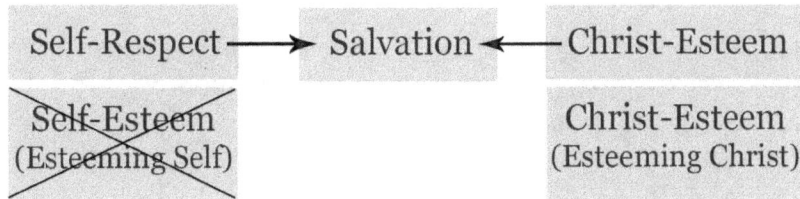

When God draws us to Himself and we acknowledge Him as Lord our God, accepting our value based on what He did, we are able to have respect for ourselves based on Him. Self-respect comes from understanding we are created in the image of God not from our behavior or our accomplishments. We now base our value on self-respect not self-esteem.

The reason our society has such little Honor being displayed or even valued today is in order for there to be Honor you must first have respect. Respect for that which you desire to Honor, a person, a position, or an institution.

This respect must have its origin in the individual giving respect before it can be rendered to another. True Honor flows out of respect from those individuals that consider respect a value to be acknowledged and defended. Many in our society do not have widespread respect for our elders, our laws, or our country's founding principles or documents such as the Declaration of Independence or the United States Constitution.

In order for there to be Honor there must first be respect, and before one can render respect a person must have respect to give—self-respect. When we are drawn to God and acknowledge Him as our Lord and Savior, the process we call Salvation, we now place value in His Word to us—Scripture.

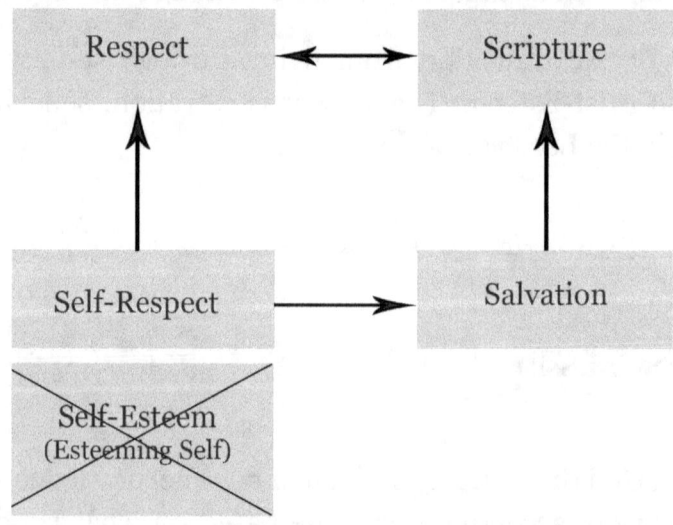

Experiencing the Grace of God, our salvation, we then acknowledge that God gave us His word, the Bible, His Scriptures. His word is where we learn the Principles and Priorities for living life. Our guide to what we should say yes or no. We now identify with Christ, we call ourselves Christian and desire to Esteem-Christ and do so by living to give Him glory.

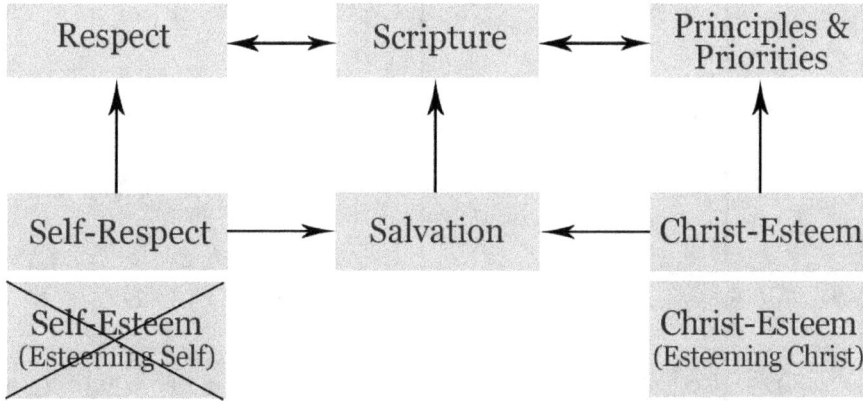

We now have standards on which the foundation of our life should be lived: Honor, God, and Worship. Our purpose is to ultimately give God glory—worship and honor Him. Consider a line drawn on paper. This line represents the beginning and end of time as God see it. Our lives are but a dot on this continuum. We see our lives through our personal perspectives, but God sees it as part of His perfect plan with the sole purpose for each of us to bring him glory.

When we see ourselves through the lens of respect, and not esteeming our value, we know our true value comes from Christ through Salvation, we respect others and live with Principles and Priorities learned from Scripture, we will be able to truly Honor and Worship God. This is when we will thrive, no longer merely existing.

Self-Respect to Worship

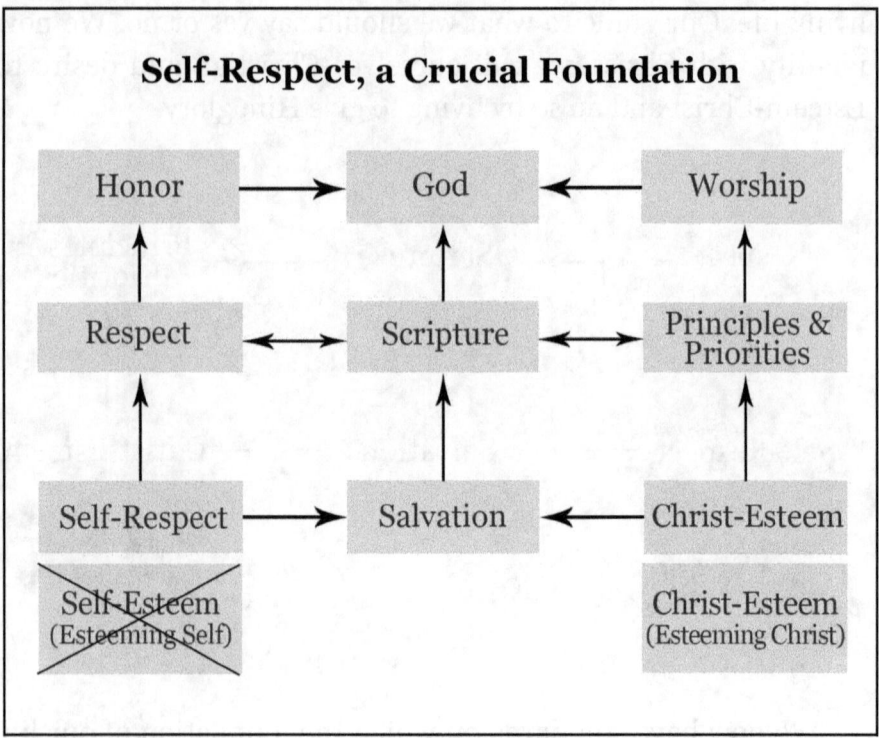

Self-respect is crucial to survive the storms of life while experiencing peace in the midst of chaos. If we base our value on anything else, when the trials of life come, and they will, we will fall apart, lose ourselves, often become angry, and our faith will most likely falter.

Chapter 12

The Journey Begins

Riding motorcycles again I am on a new journey, this time with Jodi by my side. While riding a motorcycle you see and experience things you miss while riding in a car.

When Jodi was learning to ride a motorcycle she would lead, I would follow. This was a concept a friend I ride with never considered when his wife was beginning to ride. He told me when they went riding he was constantly checking his mirrors making sure his wife was alright. I told him Jodi could see the traffic ahead more easily than what was coming up from behind. I had her six, she could concentrate on technique, not miss seeing things while experiencing the ride.

My true adventure began the year my dad died. My mom had died almost seven years earlier and now I was an orphan.

When my mother died I was still very much a hurting little boy. I did not recognize the significance of my loss. Not wanting to admit the impact it would have on my life, I remained a hurting little boy. The exact opposite was true when my dad died. I was now an orphan and could be completely honest with myself. I no longer had to protect my parents' feelings any longer.

Before the loss of both parents, the state of being an orphan was totally foreign. When you identify yourself as an orphan the reality of being a Child of God makes a huge difference. The concept of being adopted by God into His family is overwhelming yet brings peace. A peace I desperately needed and desired.

I was lost without my dad while at the same time, for the first time, free to honestly say and think about the things in life that caused harm. I no longer had to protect my parents from hurting their feelings or possibly causing a rift. I realized how lost I was, how much anger I carried, how alike I was to my brother. Despite being ten years younger, we were loving brothers, as much as either of us could love, since we were both very angry men, hurting little boys.

Having healthy relationships requires us to deal with our anger by seeking the truth about how we relate to others while learning about our motives and compensation techniques. This can be very revealing. I have learned what makes me tick, what I value and believe, and why I did the things I did.

Following the death of my dad I began to realize my anger had been triggered by the primary emotion of rejection. My dad dying caused me to experience rejection which I had never identified or dealt with before. This allowed me to begin to understand the root cause of my anger. Having shared earlier how I believed I was "damaged goods" because of my physical issues, coupled with a perception of being rejected by family and friends, brought forth the primary emotion of rejection. For many years I tried to manage until finally I dealt with my anger.

I had learned and implemented into life some very bad compensation techniques. The one I share next was the most destructive of all.

I would push those I cared for the most, the very people in my life that loved me, away from me emotionally. I would do this because of the false anticipation that they were going to reject me. My intention was to alleviate the pain of being rejected, attempting to control the situation by rejecting them before they could reject me. This was my first motive, although there was also a perceived benefit to my behavior. When I pushed someone away and that person came back I felt lovable once again. When I pushed someone away, their love for me was reinforced by them coming back. This was a selfish compensation ambition, having the person I loved reinforce their love of me. The problem with this destructive way of dealing with rejection is that every time I pushed someone away, when they came back, they never came back all the way. There was a little distance in the relationship.

Continuing this behavior over time caused the little distance created in the beginning to become a larger gap, and eventually some I had pushed away never came back. They had to protect themselves from my destructive behavior.

My brother died from a heart attack two years after my dad's death. Again opening wounds I didn't even know I had. My brother was only forty-nine years old when he died leaving a wife and three children. When I came to my forty-ninth birthday let's say it was a challenging year.

The year following my brother's death, after realizing I was an orphan after the death of my father I went to a men's conference. I had attended various conferences over the years which focused on men being better husbands and fathers. I had also attended church conferences on leadership and Christian counseling.

This particular conference brought me to my knees. I realized I had grieved God saying, "<u>Later</u>, even <u>No</u>" to the very Savior of my soul. I had lived life being comfortable by attending church, trying to live a life of honor and respect in marriage, relationships, and my profession. I focused on doing the right things, going through the motions, not being what God had called me to be. I was busy doing life, but God created me to be His child. I had been living life pursuing the things which I thought gave me value, "self-esteem," missing the self-respect I so desperately needed. I had not been willing to honestly address my fears, hurts, rejection or my anxiety. I was angry and had been trying to manage life and relationships as best I could. I was not willing to deal with the core issues. This was not always blatant or obvious but it was true, ultimately contributing to my ongoing anger issues.

The awareness of these feelings and emotions were overwhelming. This is where my strength, my ability to analyze things, became my weakness. Instead of working through the emotions that surfaced, I dove into my mind—thinking through all the ways I could make my marriage and other relationships better. Instead of being vulnerable and compassionate, I appeared distant and disengaged. I believed I was working through things by changing my outward behaviors, however I remained emotionally guarded.

The following year at another conference in a different city I was again broken. I was brought to my knees but this time emotionally broken with tears streaming down my face. The layers on my heart were being peeled back. I began to realize I had grieved my wife by not prioritizing her or our marriage. I had not been willing to be honest, vulnerable, or empathetic in our relationship. Despite this revelation, I was again too afraid to immerse myself in the feelings and emotions I was experiencing.

Through God's providence I attended another conference where I was completely emptied of myself. I realized not only had I been distant in my relationships, I was loving Christ conditionally. As long as things were going well I was able to love. God took the focus off of me and turned it toward Him. I had not just emotionally abandoned my wife, but Him as well.

In my brokenness, I was willing to explore the deeper emotions that were contributing to my destructive behaviors, my anger. I was tired of living as an angry man. I was tired of dishonoring not only my family and myself, but God. I wanted and needed to change.

This journey has taught me to embrace the God-given feelings and emotions. When I acknowledged the unresolved fear, hurt, rejection and anxiety I had ignored most of my life, I was finally able to deal with my anger, a secondary emotion. These emotions, when unresolved, limited my ability to freely love others and worship God. I have learned how to identify and appreciate these primary emotions knowing that my anger was a result of not working through what I initially felt. I am now able to be angry—sin not.

Chapter 13

Time to Retreat

For the first time in my life I intentionally got away from everyone I knew. I went on a retreat to be alone, taking time to reflect on life. I intended to consider the choices I had made because life's circumstances had brought me to my knees.

Riding with two wheels in the wind is what many call "wind therapy." Being on a motorcycle, riding without the distractions we encounter in a car, is amazing. But nothing can compare to what I experienced when I took a much needed retreat.

Never before had I taken the time to disconnect from the business of life. Never had I taken time to reflect on where I was, how I was doing, or even how I had arrived at my current state. I had never seriously considered where my life was heading. From the beginning, this retreat was just another task, or so I thought. But time of reflection requires hard work; the revelations are well worth the effort.

It was in the fall of the year my marriage was failing. I was living away from my family with a new friend who had just gone through divorce after being married twenty-two years. My step son and I had little contact, although my relationships with my three other children were loving and strong. My career was going well but now I received little satisfaction from my profession and the working relationships from which I used to gain a lot of joy.

I found a local park that allowed overnight camping. The park offered few amenities, but solitude and simplicity was what I was seeking. I borrowed a tent, sleeping bag, lantern, and camp chair. I gathered together my bible, pens and paper, a knife, and fruit and water to eat and drink. My plan was to fast—to intentionally seek God. Specifically attempting to determine what I needed to do to fix my problems.

Arriving at the park and after checking in with the Park Ranger I proceeded to get settled for my retreat. First, I gathered firewood and started a fire. Next, I setup my tent, then got organized for my stay. The campground was next to a river. I was the only one camping in the park. This was confirmed when the Park Ranger came by my campsite giving me a key to the gate. I was there by myself for the night. The ranger would be back in the morning. I watched as the Ranger drove off while experiencing the descending of silence.

The sky was clear and the stars were bright, seeming as if I could reach out my hand and grab one of the stars. The water of the river was running while the night air was cool. My senses were alive, I began to experience disconnectedness from the world. I began communing with creation.

For the next several hours I took in all I could through each of my senses: the fire with its crackle and the warmth it offered, feeling the cool night air one moment and the warmth of the fire the next while the smoke from the fire would rise and then dissipate yet the aroma was so sweet.

The river with the water rushing over the rapids and sloshing against the banks was a constant natural pacifier as my eyes became heavy, my body began to relax itself into slumber, and soon I was in a deep refreshing sleep. Something I had not experienced in a long time.

Awaking in the morning at first light, the air was much colder than the previous night. I began to shiver but soon the fire was going and warmth was once again being given off. I had planned to fast so food preparation was minimal. I only had water to drink—no coffee or juice or hot chocolate which would have tasted so good. Breakfast was water and fruit while singing praise songs. I was wakening with the park to a new day sitting by the fire for some time before taking a short hike. I wanted to experience different aspects of the park's scenery. I was intrigued by the sunrise. All the different colors and contrasts from various views in the park. The river's calming sounds continued but with the light of day the pleasant sound seemed to become lost. I worked my way back to camp and then began to address my problems. I wanted to find the formula to fix my life.

I began with a pad of paper, the bible and a pen starting at the beginning, Genesis 1:1. I was determined to work through the scriptures ferreting out the answers to my problems. Being strong-willed, determined to find answers for my life's problems, was equal to the emotional pain I was experiencing. I made my way through Genesis, Leviticus and then halfway through Numbers before taking a break. Amazingly, my note pad didn't have many notes written on it although I was more at ease. Now it was late in the morning and the fruit for breakfast was not keeping me very satisfied. I soon found myself driving my car while looking for a grocery store. Finally, I found a small community store selling some food items. Having nothing but a pocket knife I figured I would get some hot dogs and chips which would satisfy my cravings.

When I went to pay for my purchase the owner asked me what I was up to. I told him I was on a personal retreat. Cliff, the store owner, then said, "God will answer your prayers." He then told me about his personal retreat seeking answers to his life's trials the year before. How God showed up early. I left the store with anticipation of continuing my retreat.

During the drive back to the camp, I began to feel guilty about the thought of eating hot dogs and chips, breaking my fast. Coming to a four way stop in the road, there on the opposite corner was a man selling boiled peanuts. My mind was rationalizing peanuts—not a meat or fast food—relatively good for you, tasty. Now I was fasting—water, fruit, and peanuts. After I made my purchase I drove to camp and sat down at the same table where I had been studying and ate boiled peanuts without guilt. While sitting there enjoying boiled peanuts, facing the river a car drove up. I glanced over my shoulder and observed a man get out of his car and walk off into the opposite direction.

In that moment I realized my proximity to the river. The significance of water in scripture, having read earlier, how water represented life but it also represented an obstacle. I was facing an obstacle to the plans I had made when I was younger concerning life, marriage, family. I now had to choose, "a living death or a life of thriving," the choice was mine.

I had come to the conclusion that this time in my life was a chance to grow, flourish, and thrive. The choice was mine, my heart began to race.

Soon I was startled out of my thoughts, seeing the man I previously observed getting out of his car walking the opposite direction was now walking towards me. He had a walking stick in his right hand and was followed by three dogs. Exchanging greetings the stranger then proceeded to tell me all kinds of personal and bible stories, the very bible stories I had taught and used to encourage others. Stories of the people of God bringing God glory in all things.

The stranger said with confidence in closing, "We will meet again. My name is James Carroll." James left, I was dumbfounded at how I heard once again, or maybe for the first time, stories

I had read and told many times before.

The Park Ranger came to my campsite again later that evening telling him me was leaving for the night. Again, I would have the park to myself. As I settled in for the night I reflected on my day and for the first time that I could remember, my body was at ease. As the fire burned down and coolness set in I pulled the sleeping bag up settling in for another peaceful night's sleep.

I abruptly awoke at 3:00 a.m. although totally feeling rested. I realized my retreat was over, just as Cliff's retreat ended early … God so loved me that He sent one of his adopted children to remind me of what I had forgotten. God sent James Carroll—J.C.— … Jesus Christ. God gave us His word, the bible and all it contains to remind us of His love for us and that our walk isn't about us. It is all about Him. Needless to say, sleep did not resume, but I was at peace as I waited for daylight and the rising of the Sun.

I learned three very valuable lessons: First, we must be a child of God! Sounds simple but for me this was a very difficult concept to own. Having grown up believing I was expected to behave older and more mature than I was, to be a child was really foreign to me, a concept to overcome. Following my retreat I trained myself to appreciate life through the eyes of my youngest child. My youngest son at the time was just turning thirteen years old.

The second lesson learned was that I needed to trust others. Trusting others was extremely difficult for me, especially now. The one person I had trusted the most, my wife, had rejected my love and betrayed me by having an affair with one of my closest friends. The issue which I had to overcome was my mistrust of fallen man. I needed to learn to trust the trustworthy Savior.

The third lesson learned is that we can initiate a lot of things but we cannot completely anticipate or control the outcomes. I have learned to wait, most importantly to wait on God. This is exactly the opposite of what I did in my past.

My "Pearls of Life" from this retreat taught me to Be a child of God, Trust the Savior, and Wait on God. Simple, but profound.

Chapter 14

Choosing Calm

Dealing with your anger you become much more aware of bodily responses than ever before in life. Just this morning while sitting in my chair I was reflecting on how at ease, how much peace I experience, how much joy life brings. I can say with confidence I am not experiencing anger!

Each time before I get on my motorcycle for a ride I go through a mental checklist. My checklist includes my physical and mental condition, personal items and equipment, as well as the weather and where and with whom I might be riding. Every motorcyclist is encouraged to do a physical inspection of their motorcycle to insure it is mechanically sound and safe to ride.

When we truly come to peace with ourselves, any disruption to our rest will bring about a response we can learn to identify as the beginning of the anger cycle. The anger response often first shows itself as tenseness in the face with facial muscles tightening becoming much more alert.

Our stomach will most likely be the next organ to respond when we feel a tightening of our abdomen muscles, possibly some uneasiness of our stomach and some heartburn. When these symptoms are unchecked our mind will likely begin to race and dwell on specific issues—UNrest the beginning of Anger.

Now knowing anger is a symptom or a secondary emotion

being triggered by a primary emotion we are now able to mentally begin to identify and isolate the primary emotion being triggered causing us distress.

We must ask ourselves the question, "Is it Fear, Hurt/Rejection or Anxiety?"

Once we have isolated and identified the primary emotion, we must determine if what we are experiencing is legitimate. Feelings are always real just not always accurate. If it is legitimate we must further evaluate how significant the issue is and what we will choose to do, whether to drop it altogether or address the anger.

From personal experience and years of leading anger classes for men I have observed different ways people deal with their anger. Some of us, especially in the church, suppress our anger. We have been wrongly taught that anger is bad so we choose to suppress our anger.

I was the master of suppressing anger, believing anger to be wrong. I suppressed my anger so long I forgot what it was to not feel angry. Soon this choice morphed into anger repression. I was unaware of my emotional state as a result of subconsciously pushing it away. Earlier, I used the metaphor of a home where I pushed my anger way over into the corner of the room under the carpet out of sight where no one would notice I was angry. That was until one day when I opened the door and tripped over my anger causing me to fall. This is what happened to me when I realized the gravity of my anger and the need to do something about it.

Some handle anger aggressively. Surely all of us know someone with fits of rage and outbursts of anger. This is a compensation technique to mask the need for control.

Passive-aggression is a common way to deal with anger and no one even thinks we are angry. This is when our words do not match our actions, saying what we need to say in order to avoid confrontation.

Assertive anger is the correct way to handle anger, which is when we acknowledge we are angry yet we do not attack a person only their behavior and/or attitude. Jesus demonstrated this when he chased the money changers out of the temple while throwing over tables and chasing them with a whip which he had fashioned before entering the temple in order to bring reverence back to His Father's House.

The goal is to Be Angry—Sin Not. In order for this to happen we must first identify the primary emotion that has been triggered. When you feel angry, stop and ask yourself, what am I really feeling—fear, hurt, rejection, or anxiety? Then work through the pain associated with that emotion to get back to love.

Many times we get into a cycle of Anger to Love—Love to Anger because we are focusing on the secondary emotion, the symptom and not the cause of our anger—the primary emotion.

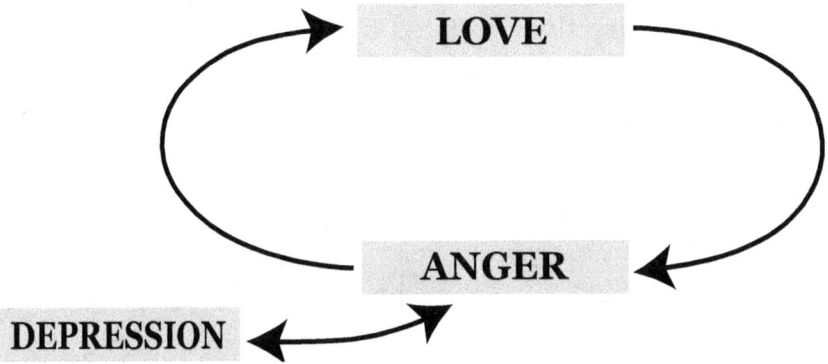

We are instructed to be angry but sin not. We are also called to be ministers of reconciliation. How can we be angry but sin not? Being angry is not the issue; it becomes sin when we attack a person. To be angry and sin not requires us to address an attitude or behavior without attacking the individual. This means that in order to deal with our anger with someone with whom we have a relationship we must reconcile—coming to an agreement that the relationship is broken. Reconciliation does not mandate renewing the relationship although we can choose to continue in the relationship—putting it back together.

Relationships, like homes, are able to be restored, renovated or refurbished. To restore something is to put it back to its original state. In relationships, it is only through Christ that this can be accomplished. To renovate a home is to remove the bad and replace it with what is good. I have witnessed many relationships thrive following a time of renovation. Two people becoming husband and wife as God intended, experiencing in-to-me-see … true intimacy.

To refurbish a home is to make the outside look good. A friend once said, "Paint covers a multitude of sins." Refurbishing a relationship seldom works because we attempt to fix what is visibly broken which is merely the symptom not the cause of the dysfunction.

Relationships are essential for life and the quality of our relationships is directly correlated to our willingness and ability to embrace our feelings, understand emotions and reason using our minds. All three are necessary to experience healthy, thriving relationships.

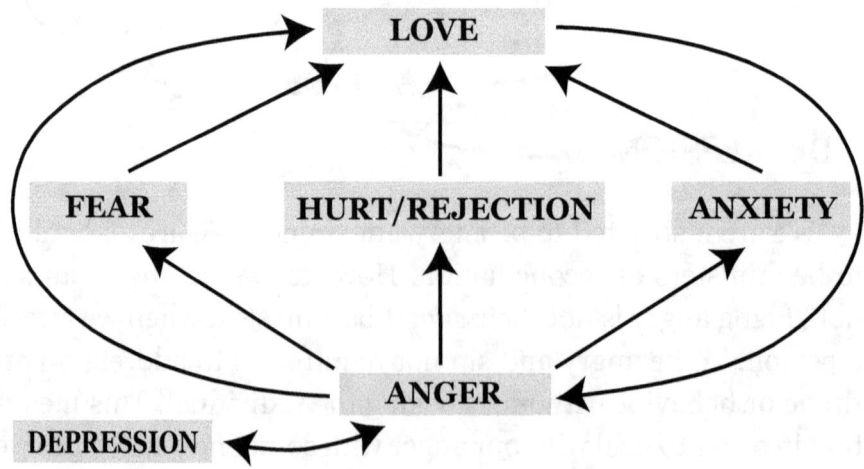

In the bible Proverbs is considered to be the beginning of the books of wisdom. In Proverbs a description is made of a youth, a young man, and man. This implies that as we grow in age we will experience seasons of life during which we will have a different focus and certainly a different perspective on which to make our decisions. We also find a focus on three words:

Wisdom, Knowledge, Understanding.

Wisdom is the acknowledgment there is a God and from this acknowledgment we are then able to love ourselves because we were created in the image of God.

Knowledge believes in absolute truth, although uncommon today, because if true we must change the way we live and what we hold as valuable.

Understanding is applying the absolute truths to our lives with the knowledge we will make mistakes.

Many Christians today do not spend much time reading or meditating on teachings from the Old Testament, although much attention is given to Paul, the Apostle in the New Testament, claiming he is "A Pharisee among Pharisees."

Reading about Paul and his life's transformation, many works and missionary journeys, I found it really difficult to identify with Paul, but found it really easy to identify with Peter.

Peter—I am. I can identify more with Peter than any other bible character.

Peter was a man who truly loved God yet his behavior got the very best of him. God so loved Peter that God gave Peter three chances to show Him his love.

Jesus told Peter he would deny Him three times before the cock would crow, a very short lapse of time. This infuriated

Peter as many of us can identify. When life happened, not the way he envisioned, Peter did deny Christ three times and following denying Christ, hearing the cock crow, Peter was devastated with remorse. Soon Christ came to Peter and offered him three chances to say he loved Him with three questions:

>**Christ:** *Peter, do you love me?*
>
>**Peter:** *Yes Lord, I love you.*
>
>**Christ:** *Peter, feed my sheep.*
>
>**Christ:** *Peter, do you love me?*
>
>**Peter:** *Yes Lord, I love you.*
>
>**Christ:** *Peter, feed my lambs.*
>
>**Christ:** *Peter, do you love me?*
>
>**Peter:** *Yes Lord, I love you.*
>
>**Christ:** *Peter, feed my sheep.*

I had done just as Peter had, seeking forgiveness and affirming my love of God. Once I reconciled with those whom I was able, "An agreement being reached," some relationships have been restored, some have not.

I learned about my love for the people of lost relationships. Just because my love was not felt or seemingly enough, doesn't mean my love was insincere or invalid. It only means my love was not received. Sadly, I loved others with everything I had at the time.

"Pearls of Life" has become our motto for a variety of accounts relating to life and life's lessons. Understanding more about pearls we can relate pearls to life lessons. A natural saltwater pearl is the result of nature and time. A lone oyster, during its mere existence, encounters a minute grain of sand. This grain of sand becomes embedded within the oyster somewhat compared to a splinter in our body. The grain of sand over time becomes a precious gem—the pearl. While inside the oyster the grain of sand, while irritating and foreign, later becomes a pearl, a beautiful, cherished, precious gem. Our pearls are those very special learnings from times in our lives marred with loss, battles and failures only later to be redeemed and used to bring glory to God.

I believe anger has become my "Pearl." Over time the anger which caused great irritation, pain and hurt has now become a precious gem. I regret the hurt I have caused others and the relationships lost. I am not able to change the past; I can make a difference in the future.

My desire and commitment is to share what I have learned with others so we might stop others from making similar mistakes. I trust you will no longer be satisfied with merely existing but truly thrive in life through vibrant rewarding and fulfilling relationships.

Afterword

Pearls of Life.net is our platform to share with others through the written and spoken word our victories from life experiences for which God is to be given the glory in all things.

We invite you to follow us on social media and join our monthly newsletter on our website.

We provide free downloadable resources, information regarding seminars, additional books we have published and guest speaking information on our website.

Website www.pearlsoflife.net

FaceBook https://www.facebook.com/PearlsofLifeLessons/

Linkedin https://www.linkedin.com/company/pearlsoflife-net/

www.ingramcontent.com/pod-product-compliance
Lightning Source LLC
LaVergne TN
LVHW051502070426
835507LV00022B/2893